"As with any unknown, the concept and reality of heaven present us with great mystery—but also great blessing. Our challenge is wrapping our brains and our Bibles around the questions. Randal Rauser's book does a beautiful job of both, guiding us toward answers to our most common questions while also helping us connect how our present lives should be influenced by those truths. I would encourage believers of any age to read this book in order to learn more about what is too often unexplored: the hope and promise of a real heaven!"

—David D. Swanson, senior pastor, First Presbyterian Church, Orlando, FL; author of *Everlasting Life*

"I love Randal Rauser because he loves to ask questions, especially hard and controversial questions. And not only does he like to ask them, but he is courageous enough to offer responses. This book on heaven follows that very pattern, and even if you do not agree with all of Randal's answers, you will find yourself enjoying how much he stretches you in the process. In the end, each of us ends up wondering how we might answer the question. Whatever your answer, it will be much more thoughtful because you have read Rauser."

—Kelly M. Kapic, professor of theological studies, Covenant College

"What a fascinating book! Randal Rauser has a wonderful way of looking at issues from a different but very interesting perspective— and he clearly does that in this volume. The questions he asks are intriguing. The answers he suggests are thought provoking. The approach he takes is engaging. This book will motivate you to think more deeply about an issue you've always wondered about: What is heaven really like?"

—George W. Sarris, actor; author; *Engaging the Culture* blogger, ChristianPost.com

What on
EARTH
Do We
Know about
HEAVEN?

What on
EARTH
Do We
Know about
HEAVEN?

20 Questions and Answers about
LIFE after DEATH

RANDAL RAUSER

BakerBooks
a division of Baker Publishing Group
Grand Rapids, Michigan

© 2013 by Randal Rauser

Published by Baker Books
a division of Baker Publishing Group
P.O. Box 6287, Grand Rapids, MI 49516-6287
www.bakerbooks.com

Printed in the United States of America

Library of Congress Cataloging-in-Publication Data is on file at the Library of Congress, Washington, DC.

ISBN 978-0-8010-1564-9

Unless otherwise indicated, Scripture quotations are from the Holy Bible, New International Version®. NIV®. Copyright © 1973, 1978, 1984, 2011 by Biblica, Inc.™ Used by permission of Zondervan. All rights reserved worldwide. www.zondervan.com

Scripture marked KJV is taken from the King James Version of the Bible.

13 14 15 16 17 18 19   7 6 5 4 3 2 1

For my dad,
who taught me to live life in the light of eternity

Contents

A Most Heavenly Equation

L ike many people, when I see an equation, my eyes tend to glaze over. So it is a matter of some irony that when I sat down to write a book on heaven, I ended up basing it on an equation. But the reason is simple: despite the potential of equations alienating an audience, they also are a powerful way of summarizing very important truths. Just consider what is arguably the most famous scientific equation of them all: $E = mc^2$. While Einstein's equation has become emblematic of erudite scientific complexity, the basic idea is actually as simple as it is amazing. The equation asserts that matter and energy, the two great kingdoms that compose everything in the universe, are not fundamentally different as common sense indicates. On the contrary, they are essentially linked. Indeed, energy is just matter in another form. Or to turn it around, matter is simply condensed energy. And under the right conditions, the one can be turned into the other.

This brings us to the one truth that most people connect to $E = mc^2$. It was the foundational discovery that made the atomic bomb possible, for an atomic bomb is simply a weapon that turns a small amount of unstable matter into enough energy to level cities. The influence of the equation, however, extends far beyond the conduct of warfare. One author explains the sweeping effect of $E = mc^2$ on our world like this:

When the Eiffel Tower is lit at night, the electricity comes from a slower reenactment of the exploding ancient atoms that took place over Hiroshima. . . . In the smoke detectors screwed tight to the kitchen ceiling, there's usually a sample of radioactive americium inside. The detector gets enough power by sucking mass out of that americium and using it as energy—in exact accord with the equation—that it can generate a smoke-sensitive charged beam, and keep on doing so for months or years on end.

The red-glowing exit signs in shopping malls and movie theaters depend directly on $E = mc^2$ as well. These signs can't rely on ordinary light sources, because they'd fail if the electricity went out in a fire. Instead, radioactive tritium is sealed inside. The signs contain enough fragile tritium nuclei that mass is constantly "lost," and usefully glowing energy sprays out instead.[1]

Think about how amazing that is. A single equation has changed our world, from the Eiffel Tower to exit signs to atomic bombs. Here's the lesson: Great equations are not irrelevant to us. Indeed, they have the potential to *transform* the world. Not surprisingly, this is a double-edged sword. While understanding and applying great equations rightly has the power to transform the way we see reality, getting them wrong, or misapplying them, can wreak untold destruction.

More Amazing Than $E = mc^2$

As amazing as it is to think that matter can be transformed into energy, the equation at the heart of this book posits an even grander linkage—one that makes $E = mc^2$ look small by comparison. You see, this equation asserts the unity of heaven and earth:

$$H = ep$$

As you may have guessed, the *H* refers to heaven. As for *ep*, that refers to earth multiplied by perfection. So the core claim of the equation that forms the central thesis of this book is that *heaven is earth multiplied by perfection.*

As I said, this is much bigger than $E = mc^2$.

It also confounds the received wisdom of many Christians who have long assumed that heaven and earth are two separate kingdoms, much like the way people used to view energy and matter. According to the heavenly equation, that's fundamentally wrong. Just as Einstein's equation asserts that under the right conditions, matter can be transmuted into energy, so according to the heavenly equation, under the right conditions—conditions that God will realize—earth can be, indeed *will* be, transformed into heaven.

I recognize that this is very different from the way many people have thought about heaven. After all, the Christian tradition has long been dominated by an otherworldly view of heaven. On the more philosophical and abstract forms of this theory, heaven is a timeless eternity—"When the roll is called up yonder, and time shall be no more"—where people eternally experience the vision of God (what theologians have often called the *Beatific Vision*).

The heavenly equation rejects the otherworldly view of heaven in favor of a *this*-worldly view. According to the equation, God's creation, like the human beings who live in it, will be transformed into heavenly perfection. It is a grand vision in which the world's future resurrection becomes the moment that spiritual, heavenly reality is incarnated in materiality. Thus the equation allows us to speak of a this-worldly heaven or an incarnate heaven. The heavenly equation summarizes this grand, transformative vision and challenges us to explore its implications for our lives and the world around us.

Twenty Questions on Heaven

As we saw, our grasp of $E = mc^2$ has transformed everything from the Eiffel Tower to exit signs to atomic bombs. If $H = ep$ is correct, then the results are certain to be even more far-reaching because it means that the very best that we enjoy of earth are glimpses of what will be transformed into heavenly glory.

Like any big idea, it will take some time to get our minds around this one. That's the goal of this book as we seek to move into understanding the heavenly equation by analyzing it from multiple angles. Our journey will begin in part 1 as we lay the foundations for all that comes after. Here we will start unpacking the meaning and significance of the heavenly equation. From there we will turn in part 2 to consider the significance of the equation for the resurrection body and the nature of our physical and emotional life in eternity. In part 3 we will address the range of ways that the natural and cultural worlds we inhabit can be redeemed for heavenly perfection. Next, in part 4 we will consider the nature of relationships in heaven by exploring our relationships with Jesus, each other, extraterrestrials (I'm serious!), and ourselves. Finally, in part 5 we will move beyond the immediate confines of the heavenly equation to ask: When the best of earth is transformed into perfection, how will it relate to the remainder, that is, hell?

I have already suggested that once we accept the truth of the heavenly equation, we can begin to see the enormous practical import of the concept of heaven. It means that the very best moments of creation provide mere glimpses of God's plan for heavenly eternity. With this in mind, I will close each chapter with three discussion questions to get us thinking more on the implications of the heavenly equation for our lives.

Heaven as the *Real*

While I've expressed the book's thesis in an equation, my background is neither science nor mathematics; rather, it is theology and literature. Since I know there are many people like me who always prefer stories to equations, let me close this introduction by providing an illustration of the heavenly equation drawn from literature.

The Velveteen Rabbit is a timeless children's book that tells the story of a stuffed toy rabbit that longs to become real. In a conversation with his close friend the Skin Horse, he discusses a question that is bursting with philosophical profundity:

> "What is REAL?" asked the Rabbit one day, when they were lying side by side near the nursery fender, before Nana came to tidy the room. "Does it mean having things that buzz inside you and a stick-out handle?"
>
> "Real isn't how you are made," said the Skin Horse. "It's a thing that happens to you. When a child loves you for a long, long time, not just to play with but REALLY loves you, then you become real."[2]

According to the Skin Horse, when a child loves a toy—*really* loves it—that love can make that toy real. And according to the heavenly equation, when God loves his creation—*really* loves it—that love transforms creation into perfection and thereby makes it real.

The thesis of this book may be an equation, but its heart is a love story, a story of becoming real. It is the story of how God so loved the world that he sent his Son to it to make it, to make us all, real.

Part 1

A World Multiplied by Perfection

Many Christians believe that God is saving them from a dying world. On the contrary, the heavenly equation claims that God is saving us *with* the world. But what does this mean exactly, and why should we believe it?

Question 1

Where Is Heaven Now?

The first Christians believed that heaven was literally located in or above the sky. In an age of science, we can believe this no longer. But if heaven isn't in the sky, then where is it?

In 1989 a major American Christian television network reported that the Soviets had abandoned a deep well in the Kola Peninsula.[1] According to the report, the trouble started when the temperature at the bottom of the well inexplicably rose to a scorching 2,000° Fahrenheit. Puzzled by the spike in temperature, the Soviets lowered an exploratory microphone into the boiling hole and were horrified to hear the chilling screams of the damned coming over the crackling reception. With terror they realized that they had drilled through the ceiling of hell!

Sometimes truth is stranger than fiction. But in this case I am happy to say that fiction was stranger than truth. The earth's core is indeed a hellish place, but not literally hell. It turns out that the whole story was a hoax.[2] Despite the fact that it was debunked long ago, it lives on as an urban legend.[3] (In the most outrageous versions, the devil is said to have temporarily escaped the hole and killed some hapless Russian oil workers.) What is truly amazing is that a major Christian television network and much of its audience took this story seriously.

While many early Christians believed hell was beneath the earth,[4] it is something of a shock to realize that some contemporary Christians apparently *still* believe it. How have modern people managed to maintain such an antiquated belief? And how do they reconcile it with those grammar-school geological maps of the earth's crust, mantle, and core?

The fact that this *hell hole hoax* has found so much traction among Christians reveals that many people have not reflected in even the most rudimentary fashion on how to reconcile their theological beliefs about the spiritual world with their beliefs about the physical world. And it presses the question: Where in our current cosmology *do* we fit hell? And that brings us to our current concern: Where do we place *heaven*?

Three Senses of Heaven

Before considering where to place heaven, we should take some time to clarify what we mean when we refer to heaven. The English word *heaven*, like its Hebrew and Greek counterparts (*shamayim* and *ouranos*), has several meanings. We will consider briefly the three primary senses: the physical sense (heaven as the sky), the spiritual sense (heaven as a present spiritual realm), and the future sense (heaven as the state of the redeemed creation).

Sky heaven. This term reflects the fact that we occasionally use the word *heaven(s)* as a means to refer to the sky, as in the sentence: "The rocket shot into the heavens." Today we treat that phrase as a convention of language, but we should remember that ancient people (including the writers of Scripture) really believed that heaven was located in the skies above.

Spiritual heaven. This heaven is the spiritual part of creation in which God's rule has existed unimpeded despite the fall. It is the realm of the dearly departed saints awaiting the resurrection. It also has at least one physically embodied resident: the resurrected Jesus.[5] Heaven as a spiritual place is reflected in the sentences, "God created the heavens and the earth," and, "Jesus ascended to be with God in heaven."

Future heaven. This phrase refers to the future, eternal reality of heaven when God's kingdom comes in its fullness. It is captured in the scriptural phrase, "new heaven and new earth," as well as the often expressed hope, "I cannot wait to experience heaven." This book is concerned primarily with this third sense, and thus when I speak of "heaven," I generally intend it in this sense, whether it is the otherworldly view that I believe is false or the this-worldly, incarnate view that I seek to defend.

In this chapter we will devote time to locating this sense of future heaven compared to the sky and spiritual senses of heaven. The relationship between heaven as the present, spiritual reality and as a future, incarnate hope for all creation is succinctly captured in Jesus's prayer, "Your kingdom come, your will be done, on earth as it is in heaven" (Matt. 6:10). This prayer expresses the desire that God's present kingdom rule in heaven (the spiritual sense) will extend fully to the earth in a process that culminates in the final state. From the perspective of the this-worldly view of heaven that is grounded in the heavenly equation, it is essentially a prayer for God to incarnate heaven in earthly form and thereby transform earth into heavenly perfection.

In Search of Heaven

For centuries many Christians assumed that hell was physically below the earth and that spiritual heaven was above it in the sky. These assumptions frame what is called the "three-storied universe"—a model that was widely held by many people in the ancient world.

One finds the three-storied universe assumed throughout the Bible. For example, in the story of the Tower of Babel, people conspire to build a tower that will reach to the heavens (Gen. 11:4). Then God comes down from heaven to see what they're up to (v. 5). The whole narrative assumes the truth of a three-storied universe. The same assumptions are evident in the New Testament. Consider, for example, Paul's description of the lordship of Christ as extending from heaven above down to earth, and even farther down to the realm under the earth (Phil. 2:10).

We certainly can't fault the biblical writers for holding to an ancient cosmology. This worldview made good sense based on the knowledge of the time, but it has not been viable for centuries. We can no longer plausibly claim that hell is in the bowels of the earth or that (spiritual) heaven is in the sky.

If spiritual heaven isn't in the sky, then where exactly is it? That question leads directly into another: Where is Jesus Christ now? This question arises because Jesus ended his ministry on earth by ascending to the spiritual realm of heaven. This made perfect sense when heaven was understood to be in the sky. But when heaven was dislocated, we were left without any place to put Jesus. Consequently, it makes sense to devote some time to locating spiritual heaven before we turn to contemplate incarnate heaven.

We can begin with the most important New Testament texts that refer to the ascension, which are found at the end of Luke and the beginning of Acts. Scholars generally consider Luke and Acts to together compose a unified work. This is significant because it means that Luke placed the ascension at the very heart of his great work.[6]

> When he had led them out to the vicinity of Bethany, he lifted up his hands and blessed them. While he was blessing them, he left them and was taken up into heaven. (Luke 24:50–51)

> After he said this, he was taken up before their very eyes, and a cloud hid him from their sight. (Acts 1:9)

The doctrine of the ascension made sense in the first-century picture of the world in which heaven was understood to be located in or above the sky. But now that we know heaven is not in the sky, where is it?

Sometimes people have tried to argue that the idea of spiritual heaven taking up space is simply passé. They point to the fact that Scripture describes Jesus as sitting at God's right hand in heaven (e.g., Mark 14:62). And they point out that "God's right hand" is not an actual place because God has no body and thus no hand, so the phrase is actually a metaphor of power and relationship that signals Christ assuming his divine rule. From that point, they conclude that if "God's right hand" doesn't take up space, and this is where spiritual heaven is, then neither does spiritual heaven take up space.

This view is right about one thing: "God's right hand" is a metaphor. But that doesn't mean that spiritual heaven has no space at all. Indeed, it *must* have space by definition since Jesus is there. Remember that Jesus's body has spatial extension (that is, it takes up space), and so it follows that heaven *must* take up space. As Wayne Grudem puts it, "The fact that Jesus had a resurrection body that was subject to spatial limitations (it could be at only one place at one time) means that Jesus went *somewhere* when he ascended into heaven."[7] So we're back to the question: If spiritual heaven must take up space, then where is that space?

Is Heaven Somewhere in the Universe?

Let's begin by considering the possibility of retaining spiritual heaven as physical space in our universe but simply shifting it a suitable distance away from the earth. In his book *The Other Side of Death*, J. Sidlow Baxter discusses various proposals of this type. For example, he recounts a group of Christians he met who believed that heaven is located on the planet Venus.[8] Baxter rightly dismisses this suggestion as completely unworkable, not least because planetologists have established that Venus, with its CO_2 rich atmosphere, is more like hell than heaven due to its surface temperatures that are far in excess of 400° Celsius (that's too hot even for those acclimatized to an Arizona summer).

Baxter then asks: "*Where*, then, are the millions of departed Christians? Have they been swept 'light years' away from earth to some 'heaven' millions upon millions of miles distant, somewhere amid those Gargantuan constellations and voluminous outer spaces?"[9] In response, he suggests locating heaven somewhere within our solar system (though he wisely opts not to venture an opinion on *where*).

Now you may be wondering: If we're going to locate heaven in the physical universe, then why does it have to be right in *our* solar system? Isn't that a bit too close for comfort? Baxter explains that this close proximity is necessary to ensure deceased souls and angels easy passage between earth and heaven. Think, for example, about the logistical problems for Samuel when he was called back by the witch of Endor (1 Sam. 28) if he had to travel all the way from the Andromeda Galaxy, three million light-years from earth.

While I appreciate why people are drawn to this kind of solution, it seems to me that locating heaven in some discrete region of our solar system is a nonstarter for a number of reasons. One very practical reason is that it implies that a well-funded NASA mission could actually *visit* heaven. Think about it: Astronauts finding Jesus in outer space? Even worse, think about the possibility of heaven tourism. Imagine if business mogul Richard Branson's Virgin Galactic[10] started offering trips to heaven! Surely that can't be possible.

So what do we do? The lesson is *not* that we should give up on the doctrine of a spiritual heaven with physical dimensions. But in terms of its location, we will have to consider models that are more radical than locating heaven in our cosmic backyard. In the remainder of this chapter I am going to consider two intriguing alternative proposals for the location of heaven that I'll call the *Another Universe* model and the *Spiritual Dimension* model.

Putting Spiritual Heaven in Another Universe

According to the Another Universe model, heaven is still understood to be a discrete spatial realm, but it is located in another universe that is completely separate from our universe and thus is safely off limits from probing astronauts and Richard Branson's space tourists. This means that when Jesus ascended to heaven, he actually left our universe altogether.

If the Another Universe model is correct, then how did Jesus get to heaven? While it is beyond our purview to speak definitively on this matter, we can consider at least one rather exotic proposal: perhaps as he was rising into the Judean sky, Jesus entered a wormhole that transported him to this other universe we call heaven.

Before going too far, we should probably explain the concept of a wormhole. The term refers to a shortcut through space-time that can allow (at least in principle) a person to leap from one point in the universe to another point, or in this case, to a completely different universe. To illustrate, think of a sheet of paper with two dots labeled *A* and *B* at opposite ends. In conventional wisdom, the quickest way to get from point *A* to point *B* is by traveling a straight line between them; however, if you curve the paper over so the two dots touch, you can then move directly from *A* to *B* without traversing the space between them. The idea of a wormhole is based on the notion that three-dimensional space is curved like that two-dimensional piece of paper so that certain points in space can be *folded over* each other and thus connect directly, like those two points on the paper.

With this model in mind, we can envision two distinct universes like two separate pieces of paper that touch at a point. The point where they touch would be the wormhole through which Jesus passed from earth to heaven.

You may be wondering: If heaven isn't above the earth, then why did Jesus even bother to ascend into the sky? Why not just enter the wormhole on the Mount of Olives and disappear? The most likely answer is *divine accommodation*. The word *accommodation* refers to the process of communicating unfamiliar concepts to a person by explaining those concepts in a way the person can understand. In this case, God wanted to communicate to the followers of Jesus that he was travelling to heaven. Since the early Christians accepted the three-storied universe, Jesus accommodated to their understanding by ascending into the sky. Then when he reached a certain point in altitude, he entered the wormhole that allowed him to pass through to heaven. Since Jesus was not concerned with providing his disciples a lesson in twenty-first-century cosmology, this was the most effective and meaningful way to depart from their presence.

Putting Heaven on a Higher Plane

This brings us to our second proposal: the Spiritual Dimension model of heaven. According to this model, spiritual heaven is a reality that overlaps the same space as the physical universe while existing at a higher dimension within it. J. Oliver Buswell suggests this model of heaven: "I do not think that heaven is any great distance away. If it were the will of God, we could see the face of our Lord Jesus Christ at any moment."[11] In this view, while spiritual heaven is part of the physical universe, it is inaccessible to our five senses. This model also has the appeal of locating Jesus physically in space without the embarrassing implication that he could be visited in heaven by a grinning Richard Branson.

In order to unpack the implications of the Spiritual Dimension model, we can turn back to the realm of quantum physics from whence the concept of a wormhole is derived. Here we find another controversial and provocative scientific notion: hyperspace or extra-dimensionality. This concept arises within string theory, which posits several spatial dimensions in addition to width, length, and height.[12]

Astronomer and Christian apologist Hugh Ross has applied this concept to a range of theological issues. For example, Ross proposes that we can explain the ability of the resurrected Jesus to disappear suddenly as well as pass through solid doors (Luke 24:31, 36) by suggesting that Christ "rotated" his body out of the three mundane spatial dimensions and into higher spatial dimensions.[13]

If this is a viable hypothesis, then it provides a fascinating possibility for the ascension. Perhaps heaven is just the realm of some (or all) of these extraspatial dimensions. This seems to allow us to have a heaven that truly is a higher realm in our midst and yet one that remains undetectable to us. In this model it could be that at the ascension Jesus *rotated* his physical body into the relevant hyperdimensions. Again, Christ's vertical ascension into the sky was simply an accommodation to first-century understandings of heaven.

While string theory continues to have many vocal critics,[14] our task here is not to work out every detail of a proposal or its possible defense but rather to survey briefly some *possible avenues* toward a solution. And it is at least reasonable to conclude that a spiritual heaven coupled with an account of its nature along the lines of extra-dimensionality could possibly hold the key.

So Where Is Heaven? And Where in It Is Jesus?

So where exactly is spiritual heaven? As intriguing as the question may be, we are simply unable to answer it at present. But the discussion has been fruitful nonetheless because it has brought out three important points.

First, it reminds us that we must be careful to avoid adopting an obsolete, ancient cosmology. This may leave us not knowing where to place Jesus, but not having an answer is better than having a patently absurd one.

Second, it underscores the importance of not spiritualizing the resurrection body of Jesus. Jesus has a physically extended, material body, and as such he must be *somewhere*, even if we cannot say where exactly that is. As we will see more fully later, this resurrection body is the down payment on the resurrection of creation—the moment at which heaven truly becomes incarnate in physical space. Heaven will one day follow Christ in becoming material and dwelling among us.

Third, the fact that spiritual heaven includes a discrete, spatially extended realm separate from our present material world places an exciting new spin on the prayer, "Thy kingdom come." It means that we are inviting the space in which God's presence is already fully manifest to colonize our space so that he may truly be all in all. Over the coming chapters we will explore the explosive significance of what that prayer entails.

HEAVENLY QUESTIONS

1. Where do you think Jesus physically is right now? Do you think it matters? Why or why not?
2. Where do you think spiritual heaven is now?
3. Why do you think some Christians have persisted in maintaining aspects of the three-storied universe despite the fact that it contradicts a scientific view of the world?

Question 2

What Does It Mean That Heaven Will Be the Earth Perfected?

The heavenly equation (H = ep) makes the extraordinary claim that the earth will be transformed into a this-worldly heaven. But what reason is there to believe this is true? Why think that heaven will one day be a perfect earth?

At some point in my youth I was taught in Sunday school that the word *Bible* can be turned into the acronym: "basic information before leaving earth." The bald message being conveyed here is that the Bible tells us what we need to know to get off this rock, not to save it. Jesus *left* the earth to prepare a place for us (John 14:3), and someday he will come back to take us there. When I was a child, I accepted an otherworldly view of heaven. At that time an equation like H = ep would have made no more sense to me than $E = mc^2$ in the age before Einstein.

Many people today continue to hold to views of heaven that are strongly otherworldly. What can be said to win their *common sense* over to the heavenly equation? In the rest of this chapter we will seek to marshal two lines of evidence for H = ep and the this-worldly view of heaven compared to the otherworldly view. To begin with, I will demonstrate how the Scriptures point toward a future resurrection of the body according to which our destiny is to exist not as disembodied souls but rather as fully incarnate beings. Further, I will point out that this incarnate existence requires the restoration of the very same body that died. As we will see, once we grant those two points, it is a surprisingly short step to extend the same logic to the resurrection of the very same world.

The Resurrection of the Body

Let's begin with the resurrection of the body. Proponents of the otherworldly view of heaven commonly believe that we become some kind of hybrid angels at death. Since I grew up with the otherworldly view, I believed that salvation was about getting your angel's wings for an eternal, ethereal existence in far-off heaven. I can't say, however, that I found that to be an appealing thought. Now don't get me wrong, I have never had any objections to angels *per se*. I think they're fine creatures (the unfallen ones anyway). Indeed, as a child I was particularly attached to my guardian angel, whom I envisioned as being 6 feet 6 inches tall, with rippling angel muscles and a shock of blond hair, and holding a flaming sword. And I was especially happy to know that my angel was leading the way on those nocturnal trips to the bathroom when bogeymen seemed to be hiding in every closet. So I definitely liked angels. I just didn't want to *become* one.

The otherworldly view of the afterlife was stated eloquently by eighteenth-century poet Alexander Pope in "On the Dying Christian to His Soul," which describes a person's soul being liberated from the body at death. The poem begins by describing the soul as a "Vital, spark of heav'nly flame," longing to leave "this mortal frame." In other words, the soul longs for liberation from the body that trammels it down. The poem then describes angels calling to the soul, "Sister Spirit, come away." As death takes the body, heaven opens and the soul cries out, "Lend, lend your wings! I mount! I fly!" The last stanza closes with a triumphant quote drawn from the apostle Paul: "O Grave! where is thy Victory? O Death! where is thy Sting?"

While I still admire Pope's literary merit, I don't accept his theology anymore. Things started to change when I was in university studying Pope's poem and decided to read 1 Corinthians 15, which provides the source for the quote in that final stanza. And there I discovered that when Paul declared, "O death, where is thy sting? O grave, where is thy victory?" (v. 55 KJV), he was *not* speaking about the soul's release from the body, as Pope implied. On the contrary, he was referring to the time when our bodies will be resurrected *just like Jesus* (see 1 Cor. 15:20–23). With growing surprise I discovered that for Paul, our future hope had little to do with the immortal soul going to heaven and everything to do with the body one day being brought back to life.

This means that we *don't* become transformed into hybrid angels at death so that we can flitter off to be with Jesus in heaven forever. Instead, God will disinter our dry bones, attach new tendons, wrap up the pulpy assemblage with fresh skin, and breathe into us to bring our very bodies back to life (including my own modest, doughy slab with the winsome smile and tousled brown hair).

The Resurrection of the World

This is big news indeed. But it raises all sorts of questions. The most glaring one is: If the body is going to be redeemed, then where will it live? Once you accept a doctrine of resurrection, an otherworldly heaven doesn't seem like an appropriate home any longer. On the contrary, a material body belongs in a material creation. And with this step, the logic of bodily resurrection leads us away from an otherworldly heaven and toward one centered on a material earth in all its glory.

The fact is that otherworldly conceptions of heaven have often lacked appeal. The timeless Beatific Vision image that I referred to in the introduction is so abstract and alien that it leaves nothing to grab on to. Little better are the popular otherworldly images that, given heaven's enduring association with the sky, have tended to come adorned with soft and blurry clouds, complemented with an innocuous palette of warm pastels. *Everything* smells like baby powder, and every solid surface is covered with crib-like bumper pads. Forget resurrection bodies; we exist in this ethereal land as flittering, disembodied spirits that resemble a collection of Precious Moments knickknacks come to life. And of course a harp is always near at hand to while away the hours. Is it any surprise that such dreary, ethereal images leave many of us pining for the best of earth?

Alas, such foreign and dreamy images give short shrift to all the goodness down here. Consider one simple example: camping in the mountains. You climb out of your warm sleeping bag and emerge from the tent into the chilly morning air. There's frost on the grass, and your breath comes out in puffs of steam. And as you look up *far* above, you can see the first rays of the sun illumining the snowcapped peaks in a pink alpenglow. "Heavenly," you whisper to no one in particular.

Indeed it is. Countless examples like this bespeak the breathtaking beauty of our world—the world we were made for. In moments like this you can do no better than quote from the psalmist as he eloquently describes the praise that creation renders to its Creator:

> The heavens declare the glory of God;
>   the skies proclaim the work of his hands.
> Day after day they pour forth speech;
>   night after night they reveal knowledge.
> They have no speech, they use no words;
>   no sound is heard from them.
> Yet their voice goes out into all the earth,
>   their words to the ends of the world. (Ps. 19:1–4)

Ultimately, if you believe that our future is otherworldly, then the resurrection just doesn't compute, for donning a physical body to inhabit an ethereal heaven makes about as much sense as strapping a fat suit on a mountain goat. But when we recognize that we were made to have a resurrection body, the natural appeal of a material existence compared to an otherworldly heaven makes good sense. Biblically speaking, the same logic that assures us that our bodies will be resurrected likewise promises the resurrection of the earth as our future home.

If we are going to grapple with *that*, we should first take a moment to outline just how pessimistic the otherworldly view of heaven is. As I said, this view often sees the Bible as a handbook for getting off earth ASAP. There's a good reason for the quick evacuation since the earth is doomed to massive apocalyptic destruction.

For a great illustration of this pessimistic picture, consider the cover of Christian heavy metal band Stryper's debut 1984 album, *The Yellow and Black Attack*. The cover shows a view of planet earth from outer space. A bluish hand (presumably God's) points at the earth, and four heavenly missiles are just about to launch, presumably to reduce the planet to a smoking postapocalyptic ruin. What a pessimistic picture of the future—the planet that God created to be our good home is going to be blitzkrieged by celestial missiles.

Once you've accepted the Christian doctrine of bodily resurrection, you can't help but begin to rethink the otherworldly picture of heaven. A nonphysical heaven simply doesn't mesh with the physicality of the resurrection body. Make no mistake, while Paul refers to our resurrection bodies as *spiritual*, that does not mean *not physical*. After all, Jesus's spiritual resurrection body, the firstfruits of ours, could eat food and could be touched. The message of the Gospels seems quite clear: the spiritual body will not be *less* than physical; instead, if anything, it will be *more physical than ever*. And if this is the case for our heavenly bodies, then shouldn't we expect it for our heavenly environment as well?

But Won't the Earth Disappear?

If the heavenly equation is to be sustainable, it needs to explain two difficult verses in 2 Peter 3 that seem to teach the destruction of the world:

> By the same word the present heavens and earth are reserved for fire, being kept for the day of judgment and destruction of the ungodly. . . . The heavens will disappear with a roar; the elements will be destroyed by fire, and the earth and everything done in it will be laid bare. (2 Peter 3:7, 10)

These two verses appear to describe creation as being destroyed in fire. Case closed?

Not so fast. To begin with, let's not miss the fact that 2 Peter 3 categorically contradicts an otherworldly view of heaven. In verse 13, Peter explains that "we are looking forward to a new heaven and a new earth." Thus, whatever else we may say, his alternative to an earth destroyed is *not* a one-way ticket to an otherworldly heaven but rather a new heaven and new earth (cf. Isa. 65:17). This picture is filled out even more in Revelation 21:2–3 with the central image of the New Jerusalem descending down *to earth* so that we may be his people and God himself will be with us and be our God. If there is going to be a new heaven and earth, then the otherworldly view of heaven is false. If the biblical writers could speak in hope of a new earth, then surely *we* ought to as well.

What about this new heaven and earth? Is it straight-out-of-the-box new? Or could it be the old heaven and earth renewed? This brings us back to the logic of resurrection, namely that the same body that dies is raised again. If God is going to restore every atom of my body, why wouldn't he likewise restore every atom of creation? And with that we come to the linchpin of our argument—an amazing section in Romans 8 where Paul explicitly discusses the *redemption* of creation in the same terms that he describes the resurrection-redemption of our bodies:

> For the creation waits in eager expectation for the children of God to be revealed. For the creation was subjected to frustration, not by its own choice, but by the will of the one who subjected it, in hope that the creation itself will be liberated from its bondage to decay and brought into the freedom and glory of the children of God. We know that the whole creation has been groaning as in the pains of childbirth right up to the present time. Not only so, but we ourselves, who have the firstfruits of the Spirit, groan inwardly as we wait eagerly for our adoption to sonship, the redemption of our bodies. (Rom. 8:19–23)

In this passage Paul argues that while creation has been subjected to the effects of the fall, it anticipates its own eventual liberation. This makes no sense if the present creation is to be destroyed and replaced by another. If you don't believe me, imagine how *you* would feel if you discovered that the Christian hope of bodily resurrection consists of the promise that after you die, someone else will be resurrected in your name. While you may be happy for that person, their resurrection will be of little consolation to you. It certainly wouldn't be your *hope*. By the same token, if creation awaits its own redemption, then it makes no sense to say the fulfillment of that hope comes in the creation of a completely new universe. And so we conclude that creation will be redeemed as surely as our bodies.

With this hope of creation's redemption in the background, we can now consider another interpretation of 2 Peter 3. In this reading, when Peter speaks of the fire that will engulf creation (vv. 7 and 10), he is referencing not a fire of destruction but rather one of *refinement*, as in Malachi 3:2–3: "But who can endure the day of his coming? Who can stand when he appears? For he will be like a refiner's fire or a launderer's soap. He will sit as a refiner and purifier of silver." With that in mind, I propose that we interpret the new heaven and earth in 2 Peter 3:13 as referring to a *renewed* heaven and earth emerging from the refiner's fire rather than a wholly novel replacement. That means that Peter is describing not the destruction of creation but rather its purification and perfection, precisely in keeping with the heavenly equation.

Heaven: Right Here Waiting

Jesus promised before he left that he is going to prepare a place for us. We have been looking for heaven over the distant horizon when all the while the place he is preparing is right before our eyes. The world around us is being prepared for the ultimate transformation into our eternal home.

It is hard to overestimate the significance of this fact. We have often thought of creation as a temporary home that can readily be dispensed with in the future as God redeems us for a life elsewhere. But if we recognize that this present home is our future home as well, it will transform our perspective on our experience in this world every day.

Think about it like this: In the otherworldly view of heaven, the earth is like a condemned house that we are temporarily visiting. With that house facing the wrecking ball in the imminent future, we would understandably extend little concern for it. But everything changes if we view ourselves as the advance crew in a team sent to restore the house to better than original perfection. Suddenly, each day we spend in the house provides further opportunity for us to work for the restoration of our eternal home.

HEAVENLY QUESTIONS

1. Have you thought of incarnate heaven as an otherworldly escape from planet earth?

2. Do you think it makes a practical difference if Christians believe God plans to save the world? If so, what kind of difference does it make?

3. Why do you think that Christians have often overlooked the promise of creation's restoration, as in Romans 8:19–21?

Question 3

Will the New Earth Include Other Galaxies?

Theologians and pastors often use the term new earth in a way that may suggest God is only saving planet earth. But God is saving the entire universe—all 130 billion galaxies.

If God is going to redeem the world he made, then it is important for us to be clear on the extent of that redemption. This brings us to two problems with the way the language of new earth is often used by pastors and theologians. The first problem is that some folks seem to limit the extent of the new earth to *planet earth*—a move that leaves the divine redemption of the rest of the universe unaddressed. I will argue that such a position is absolutely untenable and thus that we need to be clear that the term *new earth* includes much more than *planet earth*. Indeed, it includes nothing less than *everything* God created.

This leads to a second problem: Even some theologians who recognize that the term *new earth* encompasses the entire universe still often fall into the trap of using the term as if they are only referring to planet earth. The practice multiplies confusion and underscores the importance of being clear in how we speak of a redeemed heaven and earth to ensure that our speech reflects the full scope of cosmic redemption.

The New Earth as Planet Earth?

Let's begin with an example of a theologian who appears to restrict the term *new earth* to *planet earth*. Our example is drawn from Wayne Grudem's book *Systematic Theology*, which is probably the most widely used theology textbook in evangelical seminaries today. At one point Grudem discusses the vision of judgment of the earth in 2 Peter 3: "The passages . . . that speak of shaking and removing the earth and of the first earth passing away may simply refer to its existence in its present form, not its very existence itself."[1] Grudem's reference to "*its* present form" appears to interpret Peter's reference of future judgment as being restricted to planet earth.

This assumption becomes explicit as Grudem extends his analysis further by speculating on how planet earth may be judged: "Even 2 Peter 3:10, which speaks of the elements dissolving and the earth and the works on it being burned up, may not be speaking of the earth as a planet but rather the surface of things on the earth (that is, much of the ground and the things on the ground)."[2] Grudem seems to be of the view that the burning up of the earth described in 2 Peter 3 will be limited to the surface of *planet earth*, an interpretation that, technically speaking, would allow the astronauts at the International Space Station to escape the final judgment!

I must say, this is a degree of planetary specificity that I find rather hard to impute to the apocalyptic words of Peter. If Peter shared my understanding of the universe, I highly doubt he believed the apocalyptic judgment will be limited to the crust of planet earth. But don't just accept my incredulity. A little reflection reveals that Grudem *cannot* be right.

To see why, we must keep in mind that Peter's discussion of the future destiny of the earth is set against the backdrop of Genesis 1, where God creates "the heavens and the earth" (v. 1). So when Peter says, "the heavens and the earth," he is referring to the same reality that God created in Genesis 1.

Next, we note that the phrase "the heavens and the earth" in Genesis 1 is clearly intended as a catch-all phrase to encompass everything God created—the whole kit and caboodle. "The heavens" part of the component is the spiritual, otherworldly dimension of that reality, while "the earth" is the physical part. In other words, the whole physical universe is encompassed within the Genesis 1 reference to "the earth."

To underscore this point, imagine the absurdity if we assumed that "the earth" in Genesis 1 only refers to planet earth. This would reduce the grand story of creation as narrated in Genesis 1 to God tinkering with a single, obscure planet in the suburbs of the Milky Way Galaxy. The only way to avoid that absurdity is to interpret "the earth" in Genesis 1 as referring to the whole universe. But then we must do the same for references to "the earth" in 2 Peter 3. To sum up, here is my argument in three steps:

1. When Peter talks about "the earth" in 2 Peter 3, he is referring to the same reality that Genesis 1 refers to as "the earth."

2. In Genesis 1, "the earth" refers to the entire physical universe.

3. Therefore, in 2 Peter 3, "the earth" refers to the entire physical universe.

Continued Confusion about the New Earth

These days most theologians agree that "the new earth" is a reference to the entire universe. For example, Anthony Hoekema writes that "God will not be satisfied until the entire universe has been purged of all the results of man's fall."[3] Unfortunately, many of these same theologians still occasionally lapse into planetary uses of the term *the earth* that multiply confusion, and Hoekema is no exception. While he makes it clear that he believes "the earth" encompasses the entire creation, in the same chapter he also asserts, "*On that new earth* . . . we hope to spend eternity, enjoying its beauties, exploring its resources, and using its treasures to the glory of God."[4]

It appears that Hoekema is using the term *new earth* in two different ways. Sometimes it refers to the entire universe, but other times it is restricted to planet earth. Such ambiguity only perpetuates confusion about our understanding of heaven. If Hoekema is speaking only about planet earth in this sentence, then his statement is indefensibly narrow. Why think we will be restricted to spending our eternity on planet earth? Even now NASA is contemplating moon bases and missions to Mars. Will we have *less* freedom to travel and colonize the universe in eternity? And if we really will be limited to earth, what about the inevitable overcrowding problem given potentially billions of saints who will be looking for an eternal home?

The lesson is that when we speak of *new earth*, it makes a *huge* difference whether we're thinking of the entire redeemed universe or only planet earth. As a result, we should ensure that our language about the heavenly world does not restrict us to planet earth and that it avoids ambiguity that may suggest otherwise. With that in mind, we need to *recognize categorically and unequivocally that God's universal redemptive plan extends not just to planet earth but to the entire universe.* As Christians, we can accept nothing less, as texts like Colossians 1:19–20 and Ephesians 1:9–10 make clear.

Practically speaking, I propose that our default setting for interpreting references to the *new earth* be the whole universe unless a speaker specifies otherwise. Once we are clear on the meaning, we can see that the term *new earth* functions as an example of *synecdoche.* Synecdoche is the practice of using the part of something to refer to the whole. For example, if I refer to your new sports car as "a fine set of wheels," I am using a part (the wheels) as a means to refer to the entire car. Similarly, in the term *new earth*, the planet earth is being used to refer to the whole of creation.

The New Earth Is the Universe Renewed

In closing, I'm going to give us more of a sense of just how vast this difference between planet earth and the universe is.

Let's begin with the size of planet earth. Granted, the earth may not be anywhere near the biggest planet in the solar system, but neither is it small potatoes. After all, earth's mass is six sextillion metric tons.[5] And according to the estimates of demographers, as of October 2011 it is now home to over seven billion people. If you want to get a sense of just how big the earth is, I suggest you buy a ticket on Singapore Airlines Flight 21 from Newark, New Jersey, to Singapore. After 18.5 hours flying time (the longest scheduled flight in the world[6]), you will have a new appreciation for the size of our planet.

Now for some really incredible statistics. While the planet earth is big, you could fit over 1.3 million of them inside the sun. Not that the sun is particularly large by solar standards. Indeed, from a cosmic perspective it is just average. The largest known star in our galaxy, a red hypergiant named VY Canis Majoris, is so large that you could fit over *nine billion* suns within its spherical mass. And the sun and VY Canis Majoris are but two of the billions of stars in the Milky Way, a galaxy which is itself one of over 100 billion in the known universe.

Admittedly, it is impossible to get a clear grasp on the kind of scales we're talking about here. But as we struggle to grasp the immensity of the universe, we may do well to consider a 2002 image from the core of NGC 2808, a cluster of more than a million stars right in our own Milky Way[7]. The picture looks like a child shook the sand out of his swimsuit onto a black tile bathroom floor. And yet each one of these grains of sand is in fact a star. The image calls to mind Carl Sagan's famous quip that there are more stars in the universe than grains of sand on the world's beaches. Could that really be true, or is Sagan guilty of exaggeration?

Incredibly enough, it actually *is* true. According to one estimate, there are approximately 4,800 billion billion grains of sand on the world's beaches. As astronomical as that number may seem (pun intended), estimates are that with about 130 billion galaxies in the known universe, the cosmos has 52,000 billion billion stars.[8] That means that the universe has more than *ten times* the number of stars to grains of sand on the world's beaches. If anything, one could accuse Sagan of *understatement*.

All this is to say that it is no small matter to confuse planet earth with the entire universe. Not so long ago it was widely assumed that the earth was the center of things, God's crowning achievement. But no longer. As Baxter observes, "Gone forever are the days when our comparatively infinitesimal earth was thought to be the center of the universe. That this speck of solidified gas could ever be thought of as a cosmic center is now astronomically comical."[9]

If not quite comical, it surely is indefensible that Christians continue to speak as though our future home will be limited to planet earth. So let's be clear when we use the term *new earth* to specify whether we are indicating just planet earth or we are referring to everything including the earth, the sun, VY Canis Majoris, the Milky Way, 130 billion other galaxies, and all the empty space in between. As it turns out, the new earth will be incomprehensibly larger and more wonderful than we can ever imagine.

Heavenly Questions

1. When you've read the biblical references to the new earth, how have you interpreted them? Did you think they referred only to planet earth?

2. What do you think is the best way to understand the references to the new earth?

3. Do you agree that it makes a great practical difference if God is saving the whole universe? If so, what is most significant to you about that fact?

What Is God Saving the Universe From?

The cosmos may not be alive, but it is dying just the same, decaying from the inside as it marches inexorably toward what cosmologists call the heat death of the universe. But that's not the end of the story. Just as God will one day redeem us from our own bondage to decay, so he will redeem the universe.

I read dozens of novels as a child, and many of them had a lasting impact on me. But I doubt that any touched me as deeply as H. G. Wells's haunting science fiction story *The Time Machine*. This famous novella is set in Victorian England. Or at least that is where it begins. Narrated by a man who is simply identified as "the Time Traveller," the book tells the story of his journey into the distant future.

As the story opens, the Time Traveller builds a time machine that whisks him to "the year Eight Hundred and Two Thousand odd."[1] When I read that date at the age of ten, I remember my mind reeling at such an unimaginably distant year. When the Time Traveller arrives in the distant future, he discovers not only that contemporary (Victorian) England has long since disappeared, but so have Homo sapiens, because our species has since evolved into two distinct species: a worker class called the Eloi, and an exploiting class called the

Morlocks. (For those who are interested, the story functions as an allegory of Victorian class struggle.)

The simple story of *The Time Machine* haunted me at several levels. To begin with, there was the tragic portrait of the Time Traveller's ill-fated relationship with the Eloi and their hopeless struggle against the Morlocks. At a deeper and more fundamental level, I was disturbed to contemplate the disappearance of Homo sapiens from the world. Could there really be a day coming when our species will disappear from the scene altogether?

But for me the most existentially disturbing dimension of the story centered on Wells's description of planet earth in the distant future. Near the end of the book, the Time Traveller leaves AD 800,000 in the distant past on a quest millions of years on into the future to discover the ultimate fate of the universe. Reading the book as a child, one passage in particular stuck in my mind, and here I'll let the Time Traveller tell his own story:

> So I travelled, stopping ever and again, in great strides of a thousand years or more, drawn on by the mystery of the earth's fate, watching with a strange fascination the sun grow larger and duller in the westward sky, and the life of the old earth ebb away. At last, more than thirty million years hence, the huge red-hot dome of the sun had come to obscure nearly a tenth part of the darkling heavens. Then I stopped once more, for the crawling multitude of crabs had disappeared, and the red beach, save for its livid green liverworts and lichens, seemed lifeless.[2]

Lifeless. The thought that all life will one day disappear as the world slowly marches toward complete annihilation chilled me to the core of my being. Could the future of everything really be . . . nothing?

Since Wells published *The Time Machine* in 1895, our scientific understanding of the universe has grown in ways that nobody could have anticipated. In particular, our grasp of the scale of space and time has increased multiple orders beyond anything in Wells's wildest imagination. While we used to think the Milky Way was the universe, we now recognize that it is merely one of *billions* of galaxies. Wells was equally far off when it came to time scales. He described the Time Traveller encountering the sun as a red orb thirty million years into the future. As incomprehensibly distant as this may seem to us, *he actually underestimated the time involved by more than a hundredfold*: current estimates are that the sun will not become a red giant for another *five thousand million years*. Right across the spectrum, our understanding of the size and age of the universe has increased exponentially.

Despite our much greater understanding of the universe's size and age, from a cosmologist's perspective, one thing hasn't changed: The future still looks hopeless. In fact, it now looks bleaker than Wells ever imagined. Just how bleak? As a thought experiment, let's explore the current cosmological projections for the future of our universe in our own imaginary, alternate, future time machine. *And please keep your hands inside the machine at all times; we certainly don't want to leave any limbs in an alternate future.*

A Journey into a Hopeless Future

I grasp the ivory handle and pull down the brass lever. The machine begins to whir, we hear a click and a wheeze, and then we begin to spin slowly. The spinning quickly gains intensity as the environs around us are reduced to a blur and the dials begin to spin: 800,000 years . . . 30,000,000 years. . . . Finally at 1,000,000,000 years into the future I snap the brass lever back and the machine's spin begins to decrease.

The dials slow, and with a final click the year pops up: AD 1,000,004,321. The air is scorching hot. There is no liverwort or lichen growing on *our* rocky beach. And there certainly is no ocean. I look over at you. "The oceans boiled off long ago due to the sun's increased solar output," I explain. "Needless to say, all life went extinct eons ago." Even though we started off near Dover, England, a temperate climate in our day, the landscape now feels as hot as a sauna and could pass for the waiting room of hell. I look at you and grin. "You think this is bad?" I say. "Well this is nothing. Wait till you see what the future has in store."

With that I slam the brass lever down again and the scene of desolation is reduced to a blur. As we begin to spin into the future I flip two switches. "The first switch ignites the levitating engines ensuring that we're nowhere near the ground when we stop." You give me a questioning look so I add, "You'll see why in a moment. As for the other switch, it maintains our microclimate. That will protect us from being instantly incinerated by the heat."

At that moment I yank the lever back up again. The spinning dials slow, and with a click the machine reads the year AD 3,234,053,090.

The levitating engines are keeping us hovering well above the surface of the earth, and it is a good thing too. While the sun hangs above us, a giant, sullen red orb taking up more than a tenth of the entire sky, the surface of the planet below has been reduced to molten rock for as far as the eye can see.

The closest thing you can compare it to is some footage you saw once of the Mauna Loa lava flow in Hawaii. But that is a mere campfire compared to this tortured ocean of perdition. "It looks like the lake of fire," I muse. You strain to hear me over the roar of the super-duper air-conditioning unit. "If that wasn't running," I shout gesturing toward the blasting vents, "we would already have been vaporized by the heat." Despite the air-con, it is quickly getting intolerably warm. And with that I push the brass bar—now almost too hot to touch— back down, and we begin to spin out of this terrestrial hellhole and on farther into the future.

All around us the spinning blur gradually takes on a deep, fiery red hue as the dials whir at a dizzying speed. Then the color turns progressively brighter until we are forced to shield our eyes from the blinding glare. *"That's the sun consuming the earth!"* I yell over the thunderous roar created by the whirling machine and the passage of billions of years. "We're now continuing onward into the future for a glimpse of the heat death of the universe!" The term *heat death* is liable to be misunderstood, for it is not a death *by heat* but rather the death *of heat, of movement, of order,* and most certainly *of life.*[3] On the best projections, it represents the bleakest, unimaginably distant future for our universe.

And when will that be? After an unimaginably long span of time I snap the lever up and the rate of spinning begins to decrease. As the dials slow, you do a double take. Were there that many dials to begin with? You certainly don't recall. But now in front of you are dozens of dials spinning as the year clicks into place. The time is impossibly distant. We have arrived at AD 1,000,000,000,000,000,000,000,000,0 00,000,000,000,000,000,000,000,000,000,000,000,000,000,000,00 0,000,000,000,000,012,345,050,400,345.

At this point the problem is not the heat. Rather, it is the un-imaginable cold. The super-duper heaters of our time machine are now roaring at full blast, struggling to maintain our precious mi-croclimate against a temperature that is mere billionths of a degree above absolute zero, which is −273.15°C or −459.67°F. I look over at you and explain, "All the stars, black holes, and gasses have long ago dissipated to nothingness as the universe has continued to expand. There is now no thermal energy left. Everything is perfectly uniform. The once vibrant universe has become cold and dead." With that I pause for a moment to gaze into the nothingness that pushes in all around us, a universe unimaginably darker, blacker, deader, and bleaker than the bottom of the deepest coal mine. "But we can't stay here long," I add hastily, as we feel the frigidity snaking in all around us. "If we don't leave now we're liable to turn into a Bose-Einstein Condensate any moment. And take my word for it, you don't want that!" With that I solemnly push the lever down once again. Back we go. In the blur of traversing trillions and trillions of years back to the present, we see light emerge once again, then the sun and earth return, and at long last, the rustling leaves, twittering birds, and blue sky of the present.

A Future Not Our Own

This thought experiment describes a future of the universe, but it is not *our* future. Rather, this bleak account of heat death describes an alternative heat-death future that will occur *except for the great divine interruption*. God is going to intervene in the slow slide to ultimate decay. He will turn back the arrow of entropy once and for all and heal his dying world.

So the Time Traveller in H. G. Wells's classic story wasn't just wrong about the size and future of the universe; he also got its destiny wrong. If we were allowed a glimpse into that unimaginable future, we would see not a red beach reduced to liverwort and lichen, still less a universe fading away to nothingness. On the contrary, we would find that the old order of things will one day disappear as the beach and its environs come to life with beauty and abundance heretofore unknown in all creation as the heavens and earth praise God in glorious harmony.

I will never forget the images of *The Time Machine*. By painting such a bleak portrait of the future, Wells gave me a vivid sense of the mortality from which God is saving the universe. Wells's calculations are not simply off by an order of magnitude. They are completely wrong because he didn't include the Creator in his calculations—the one who will one day act to redeem this dying world from its own mortal fate.

Heavenly Questions

1. How would you feel if you believed that H. G. Wells accurately described our future?

2. Do you think it is helpful to see God as saving the universe from its own mortal decay?

3. Does this change the way you view the universe now?

Question 5

Will We Recognize the Earth When It Is Renewed?

If God is going to resurrect the same universe, then we can expect to recognize it. As for planet earth, it is reasonable to expect to find many of the same landmarks, including familiar lakes, islands, and cities. Does that mean we will still be able to visit Tahiti?

I have my own bucket list of places I'd like to visit before I die. My bucket list contains a number of desirable destinations like Florence (home of the Italian Renaissance), Machu Picchu (that mysterious abandoned city high in the Andes Mountains), and the Egyptian pyramids. While it initially seemed like a good idea, I soon found that once you start a bucket list, you keep on thinking of new destinations to add. And so my list quickly grew. Soon the original list of seven choice destinations (inspired by the Seven Wonders of the World) grew to ten, then fifteen, and eventually twenty. By that time things were starting to get a little absurd.

It is at this point that H = ep took on an enormously practical resonance, for it meant that I could whittle my primary bucket list back down to the manageable number of seven destinations and relabel it the *present-life bucket list*. Then I could place all the leftovers on a secondary *next-life bucket list* that will be devoted to places I could visit after my resurrection. And the best part: since I will have an eternity to explore, there need be no limits on the second list.

Does a Resurrected World Mean a Resurrected Tahiti?

At present, the number-one entry on my next-life bucket list is the tropical paradise of Tahiti, the hub of French Polynesia cradled in the South Pacific, protected by shoals of coral and crowned by beautiful mountains.

Does this all sound a bit weird? Well the idea of a next-life bucket list is not as fanciful as you may think. In fact, it helps us focus on important questions about the continuity between the universe now and after its own resurrection. But is the continuity as great as my next-life bucket list assumes? That is, will I really be able to visit Tahiti in the next life?

Let's begin by noting that the Israelites seem to have understood the new creation to maintain substantial continuity with the present order of things. That's why they described the New Jerusalem as standing at the center of it (Isa. 65:17–19). The restoration of such familiar places suggests the redemption of the world in recognizable continuity with its present form. If a New Jerusalem will be there, it is not unreasonable to expect (or at least hope) that a new Tahiti will be as well.

We can pursue this further by carefully considering the close analogy between created and redeemed human persons on the one hand and a created and redeemed creation on the other. In the case of Jesus—the firstfruits of the resurrection—the very same person who died was raised again. As if to underscore the point, John notes in his Gospel that the postresurrection Jesus had the very same wounds in his hands and side as Jesus had on the cross (John 20:27).

Based on this, Christians commonly assume that there will be recognizable continuity between the body that dies and the form in which it is resurrected. As Daniel R. Lockwood observes, "If we can recognize the Lord Jesus, possessing the perfectly restored and glorified bodies to do so, it follows that we will recognize other believers, including our loved ones."[1] Many Christians assume that this same degree of continuity will be present in other resurrected persons, for they expect to see and recognize loved ones in eternity.

Christians also reflect these assumptions about recognizable, bodily continuity when they talk about who they'd like to see in heaven. One gentleman says, "I'd love to speak with Moses." A woman adds, "I'd like to ask Mary if Jesus ever talked back as a child." And then the emergent church guy jumps in: "I can't wait to kibitz with Martin Luther over a pint of good German beer." While such statements may strike us as fanciful, at the very least they reflect an assumption that we will be able to recognize specific individuals in heaven. If we can reasonably expect one day to pick out Martin Luther in the streets of the New Jerusalem based on the Cranach portrait that we once saw in a history book, then why shouldn't we expect to recognize Tahiti based on the picture we saw in a Lonely Planet travel guide? If our resurrection bodies will represent a reasonable facsimile of the body that died, why shouldn't we expect the resurrection of creation to do so as well?

A Deeper Country

C. S. Lewis provides a fascinating reflection on the resurrection of creation in the final volume in the Narnia Chronicles, aptly titled *The Last Battle*. The scene unfolds as the Pevensie children are entering what *appears* to be Narnia, except that, curiously enough, it seems to be *more like Narnia than Narnia ever was*. We join the passage in progress with Lucy making an observation about the distant hills of this new land:

> "But look there." She pointed Southward to their left and everyone stopped and turned to look. "Those hills," said Lucy, "the nice woody ones and the blue ones behind—aren't they very like the Southern border of Narnia?"
> "Like!" cried Edmund after a moment's silence. "Why they're exactly like. Look there's Mount Pire with his forked head, and there's the pass into Archenland and everything!"
> "And yet they're not like," said Lucy. "They're different. They have more colours on them and they look further away than I remembered and they're more . . . more . . . oh, I don't know."
> "More like the real thing," said the Lord Digory softly.[2]

How right Lord Digory is. The new Narnia is not simply Narnia replicated or refurbished. Rather, it is Narnia made more real than it ever was before. The narrator tries to explain the new Narnia with an illustration drawn straight from Plato's Allegory of the Cave:

> You may have been in a room in which there was a window that looked out on a lovely bay of the sea or a green valley that wound away among mountains. And in the wall of that room opposite to the window there may have been a looking-glass. And as you turned away from the window you suddenly caught sight of that sea or that valley, all over again, in the looking-glass. And the sea in the mirror, or the valley in the mirror, were in one sense just the same as the real ones: yet at the same time they were somehow different—deeper, more wonderful, more like places in a story: in a story you have never heard but very much want to know. The difference between the old Narnia and the new Narnia was like that. The new one was a deeper country: every rock and flower and blade of grass looked as if it meant more. I can't describe it any better than that: if ever you get there you will know what I mean.[3]

The new Narnia is not a new country. Instead, it is the old Narnia made new: deeper, brighter, more real than ever before. All the old glorious places are there—the mountains, plains, seas, and castles—but they are all now perfected.

Thinking about Tahiti

Let's explore this idea a bit more by focusing on that first entry on my next-life bucket list. Imagine that Christ comes back in 2020 to establish his kingdom. At the time Tahiti boasts scenic mountains, beautiful beaches, famous roiling surf, and the quaint city of Papeete, the administrative capital of the region, nestled on the coast. Then the curtain drops on Tahiti and the rest of the universe and a sign goes up declaring, "Closed for renovations." When the sign is taken down and the curtain is pulled back, we see a creation resurrected in fullness to new life, more like the real thing than ever before. If creation will be resurrected to new life, then why shouldn't we expect Tahiti to be there too with all its mountains, beaches, surf, and towns still recognizable but more real than ever?

If there is a resurrected Tahiti to visit, how will I get there? Will human technology still be operative? If so, then maybe we will fly modified Boeing 787 Dreamliners with crystal bottoms that provide a full view of the passing scene, seats that fully recline, and of course no more air-sickness bags. Or perhaps airplanes will be rendered otiose by teleportation chambers. "Beam me over to Tahiti please!"[4] My favorite option, however, is that our resurrection bodies may have the ability to fly. Imagine hurtling along over the Pacific as the sun sets in the west and the stars turn on one by one overhead.

Arriving in Tahiti

In the distance I can see the sparkling lights of Papeete dancing on the waters. As I arrive I'm filled with questions. How much has Tahiti changed? Are the mountains the same but with more colors? Do they look farther away? Are they more like the real thing? And what about the city of Papeete? Have all the toilets been turned into planters and the police stations into community centers? And are most of the residents still Fijian natives, or has the island been overrun by resurrected Scandinavian and Canadian tourists who, like myself, spent too much of their previous life in snowy climes wishing for an extended vacation such as this? (Good news for the sun-deprived and fair-skinned Scandinavians and Canadians: our pale, northern skin will no longer be susceptible to sunburn!) Do the Tahitians still speak French? If so, will I be able to converse with them with all the eloquence of François Mauriac? And where am I going to stay?

Ah, but those are questions for tomorrow. After all, I just arrived. I stretch out on the cool sand as the palm trees sway overhead in the evening breeze. The stars definitely seem brighter, the salty air sweeter than any I can remember. I praise God for his creation as I pull out my list. Tahiti, *check*. I look over the rest of the list: Mt. Everest, Easter Island, Guam, Sicily, Victoria Falls, Stockholm, Shipton's Arch, and so many more. My heart fills with anticipation.

Then as I turn back to the night sky, a thought occurs to me. My next-life bucket list is completely limited to terrestrial destinations. "What about the rest of the universe?" I say aloud to no one in particular.

All sorts of new possibilities crowd my head: the mysterious seas of Jupiter's satellite Europa; an exhilarating pass by the sun; a journey out to the lonely space of the Oort cloud at the edge of our solar system; and then an extended vacation at that massive black hole at the center of the galaxy that I once read about in *National Geographic*. The possibilities are endless. But they are destinations for another day.

As the sky's final shades of purple turn to black I stand, brush off the more real sand, and turn back to focus on the lights of a more real Papeete—a glowing jewel set against the darkened hills, luminescent and welcoming as the tropical night closes in. As I walk toward the city I can just hear a beautiful sound dancing over, in, and woven through the evening breeze. It's the song of Psalm 19. Creation is singing softly and at peace. It's hard to describe. You'll know it when you hear it.

Heavenly Questions

1. Do you think that the presence of Jerusalem in the new creation makes it plausible to think Tahiti will be there as well?

2. Do you find the idea of a next-life bucket list appealing? Which destinations would you place on such a list?

3. What about horrible places like Auschwitz? Would the new creation be better off if such places disappeared altogether? Or do you think that God will redeem even places that have seen great evil?

Part 2

Perfect People in a Perfect World

As we saw in part 1, the promise of resurrection provides our hope for eternity. In part 2 we are going to focus on some aspects of the perfected human body and community. What will it mean for the rather unimpressive human specimens we see every day—and alas, often in the mirror—to be perfected?

Question 6

How Old Will We Be—and Will We Get Older?

Theologians have typically assumed that the age of resurrection bodies will be uniform—we'll all be resurrected at the same age and we will never grow older. But these assumptions are not without cost, for a world in which everyone remains the same age is a world that has surrendered the richness of a community with people of diverse ages who grow older through time.

When I was a teenager I thought I was pretty much invincible. I blush to admit that this erroneous assumption occasionally resulted in inexcusably reckless behavior, such as passing cars on a blind corner and cliff jumping into unknown waters.

Despite the occasional dally into foolishness, I made it into my twenties more or less unscathed, by which time I had grown significantly more sensible. That sensibleness was rooted in the fact that by then I recognized that I was not invincible and thus that reckless behavior could have serious repercussions.

If my twenties represented my belated recognition that I was not invincible, my thirties brought me face-to-face with the fact that I shared the same terminal diagnosis as all other human beings. I call it HMS (human mortality syndrome), and it has a 100 percent mortality rate. Of course I always knew I was going to die, but there's a difference between knowing and *knowing*. There was something about hitting the big 3-0 that for the first time led me to contemplate my mortality from an existential perspective I had not considered before. Around this time the opening stanza of Robert Herrick's "To the Virgins, to Make Much of Time," a poem I had studied in university, came back to haunt me:

> Gather ye rosebuds while ye may,
> Old Time is still a-flying;
> And this same flower that smiles today,
> Tomorrow will be dying.

Though I had once seemed immortal, I could no longer deny the fact that I was slowly dying and there was nothing I, or anyone else, could do about it. As difficult as this sobering realization was to accept, it had one positive benefit: it prompted me to consider more carefully my theology of the resurrection body, including very practical questions concerning the age of our bodies and whether we will grow older.

Thomas Aquinas on Resurrection Age

One of the most influential discussions of the age of the resurrection body comes courtesy of Thomas Aquinas in his *Summa Theologiae*.[1] Aquinas begins by considering the argument that those who die when they are elderly will be resurrected with elderly bodies. Since he lived in a time when the elderly were highly respected, it didn't make sense for them to give up that respect for a youthful resurrection body. Next, he considers a very different argument that claims the essence of personhood is most fully manifested in childhood, and thus concludes that childhood resurrections should be the norm.

Aquinas rejects both options. Instead he argues that we will be resurrected at youthful age that he believes is perfectly represented in the resurrection body of Christ. In support of this claim, he appeals to Ephesians 4:13: "Until we all reach unity in the faith and in the knowledge of the Son of God and become mature, attaining to the whole measure of the fullness of Christ." Aquinas argues that this passage describes not only spiritual maturity in Christ but also physical maturity. From this he concludes that we will be resurrected at the ideal age of bodily maturation that was perfectly manifested in the resurrection body of Jesus Christ.

This begs the obvious question: At what age was Christ resurrected? In his discussion, Aquinas follows Augustine in identifying this youthful age as being approximately thirty years old. Elsewhere, in his *Catechism*, he identifies what he calls "the perfect age" as being "thirty-two or thirty-three."[2] So it appears that Aquinas takes the position that we will be resurrected at the same age as Jesus's resurrection body, that is, at thirty-two or thirty-three.[3]

Aquinas's belief that Jesus was resurrected at the age of thirty-two or thirty-three is presumably based on the assumption that Jesus was born in the year AD 1 and crucified in the year AD 33. While it is likely that Jesus was crucified in AD 33, he definitely wasn't born in AD 1. We know this because Herod the Great, a major player in the narrative of Jesus's birth, died in 4 BC. Consequently, Jesus could not have been born any later than 4 BC, and he could have been born as early as 7 BC.

If you calculate the age of Jesus based on these numbers, you have a resurrected Savior who was no younger than thirty-four and could have been as old as forty, *not* the comparatively young thirty-two or thirty-three that Aquinas assumes. If Jesus provides the template for our resurrection, then it means that we too will be resurrected somewhere between the age of thirty-four and forty. Who would have thought that a *youthful* resurrection body may be *pushing forty*?

This presents a problem for Aquinas given that the mid- to late thirties do not represent the human physical peak. According to physiological studies of the human body, the physical peak typically occurs more than a decade earlier—in the early twenties. As Lewis R. Aiken observes, "This is when they are stronger, quicker, healthier, sexier, and their bodies are generally at a higher performance level than at any other age."[4] In fact, depending on what measure we use to identify a peak, the age may be even younger. For example, Aiken points out that the heart and respiratory systems reach their maximum effectiveness in *late adolescence*.

Whichever way you look at it, the evidence is overwhelming that a body in its mid- to late thirties is already well on its way to physical decay after peaking in the late teens to early twenties. Consequently, if we are all resurrected at the age Jesus died, and Jesus was resurrected with a body aged between thirty-four and forty, then we will inherit a body that is already in significant decline.

Growing Older in the Kingdom?

Aquinas's discussion of age reflects two key assumptions that have typically framed the way theologians address the age of the resurrection body:

> *Uniform age assumption*: resurrected bodies will all be the same age.
>
> *Static age assumption*: resurrected bodies will not grow older.

While these are deeply rooted assumptions, they are not beyond question. Consider, for example, Isaiah 65:20—a messianic passage that offers a memorable glimpse of the heavenly age:

> Never again will there be in it
> an infant who lives but a few days,
> or an old man who does not live out his years;
> the one who dies at a hundred
> will be thought a mere child;
> the one who fails to reach a hundred
> will be considered accursed.

This description of God's kingdom contradicts both the uniform and static age assumptions. It depicts the redeemed human community as consisting of a variety of ages, extending from infancy to the elderly, with people growing older through time. Does this passage provide us with adequate warrant to rethink these venerable assumptions?

Before we get too excited, we should note a rather glaring problem with simply adopting Isaiah 65:20 wholesale into our picture of heaven: it depicts people *dying*. Certainly we cannot countenance *that* possibility if we accept with Paul that we will be raised immortal (1 Cor. 15:52).

We can conclude, then, that if we reject the depiction of people dying in the passage, we should likewise reject the rest of the passage's portrayal of a community of diversely aged and aging persons. But this needn't follow. We could accept the general picture painted here of a diverse community of people who grow older without accepting every detail, including the problematic description of people dying. We should keep in mind that the emphasis of the passage is not that people will continue to die but rather that they will live extraordinarily long. Based on this, one could in principle continue to affirm the passage's theme of longevity by extending the logic out further and concluding that people will *never* die. And one could do this while still using the passage to reject the uniform and static age assumptions.

But does this idea of immortals aging even make sense? As we address this question, it may help to take a step back and ask why theologians have tended to assume that the age of resurrected persons will be uniform and static. No doubt the belief in uniformity is undergirded by the assumption that Christ's resurrection body is the firstfruits of all subsequent resurrection bodies (1 Cor. 15:20). And it is natural to extrapolate from this that our resurrection body will share the age of our resurrected Lord. As for the static nature of that body, this follows naturally from the assumption that the body will live forever. To be sure, we need not believe that the body will be *completely* static; for example, presumably our hair and fingernails will still grow. But given that aging is a sign of *mortality*, if you are going to live forever, it seems to follow that you can age no longer.

The Case for Aging in Eternity

These are decent reasons to accept the uniform and static nature of resurrection bodies, and they may seem to be sufficient to trump the remaining details in the vision of Isaiah 65:20. But before we render final judgment, we should consider some arguments in favor of an aging community.

To begin with, aging adds a dimension of richness to an individual's life experience. Each stage of life has its own beauty and value, and that includes old age. As W. Somerset Maugham poignantly observed, "Old age has its pleasures, which, though different, are not less than the pleasures of youth."[5]

Further, a community with a diverse and aging population reflects a richness that is simply not present in a community with a population of uniform and static age. These days it is a recognized truism that gender, ethnic, and cultural diversity all contribute to the richness of a human community. The same principle applies here: age diversity in a community provides a richness that is not present when everyone is a uniform age. In his book on community development, Timothy Beatley critiques the "age-truncated and overly narrow age-focus" of contemporary communities. He observes, "A genuine place, a place that feels real and authentic to us, is a place . . . that is diverse, and this must necessarily include age diversity."[6] Beatley goes on to list several values of having representative age diversity in a community. Although not all of them would be of value in heaven—for example, the value of learning to protect and care for the vulnerable—other aspects of age diversity would enrich a society of immortal peoples. The more you think about it, the more diverse age emerges as a value well worth defending. For point of analogy, compare a reforested plot of uniform, ten-year-old saplings with the rich biodiversity present in an old-growth forest replete with trees ranging from nascent saplings to towering thousand-year-old monoliths. Undoubtedly the former lacks the rich diversity of the latter. Consequently, just as we would not want to lose the diversity of gender, ethnicity, and culture in a community, neither should we want to lose the diversity of age.

In addition to a diversity of ages, the *process* of aging also brings a richness that would be lost if our resurrection bodies remain statically locked at a particular age. Change over time adds to the excitement and interest of life. If you don't see your friend's children for five years, it is exciting to see how much they've grown. And it is poignant to see the wrinkles and gray hair that have been added to your friend's own visage.

But wait. Aren't wrinkles and gray hair signs of the perishability from which we seek to be delivered? How can resurrected immortals show signs of aging any longer?

The problem, in my view, is not with the acquisition of gray hairs and wrinkles per se. Rather, it is with the twofold fact that this process of aging is irreversible and terminates in death. But if those two facts are removed—as they surely will be for an imperishable person—then the acquisition of gray hair and wrinkles will no longer serve as sobering reminders of one's imminent demise and can instead be accepted as natural stages in the eternal aging process.

Assuming that human beings do age in eternity, what would that look like? Presumably it would mean that people go through natural regenerative cycles of growing older and then younger again. It may be that we will grow older until we reach a particular age, perhaps the equivalent of seventy earth years. Needless to say, if we did grow to seventy, it would be the most athletic and spry seventy-year-old body imaginable—one free of the common blights of mortal aging like osteoporosis and arthritis while embodying that elusive quality of growing old with grace.

Whatever the threshold of age may be, once it is reached, people will grow younger again. It may be that this growing back into youth could occur in real time, as it does in the film *The Curious Case of Benjamin Button*. It strikes me as more likely, however, that the reversion to youth occurs in an instant—the proverbial "twinkling of an eye"—at which point we begin the cycle of aging again. But it is tough to be dogmatic on this point given the highly speculative nature of the discussion.

In case you think I've gone off the deep end, I grant that the whole idea of cyclical aging in eternity may sound rather fantastic. But it is surely no more fantastic than the idea that a body that rotted into the earth millennia ago will suddenly be restored to perfect life. If the omnipotent God can resurrect a body—as he surely can—then he can also create an enriched, human community of diversely aged and forever aging, immortal persons.

It may be that in this way we find a healthy balance between the desire for a diverse redeemed community with the rhythms and glories of aging but shorn of the shadow side of mortality. In a refurbished Herrick:

> Gather ye rosebuds for each day,
> Old Time is ever flying;
> And this same flower that smiles today,
> Is aging but never dying.

HEAVENLY QUESTIONS

1. Do you think there is an optimal age to be resurrected? If so, what is it?
2. Do you agree that a diversely aged population enriches a community? If so, is that a sufficient reason to think that eternity will have a diversely aged, and aging, population?
3. Do you prefer that your resurrection body undergo cyclical aging or that it remain at the same age?

Question 7

Will We All Be Beautiful?

On this side of eternity, some of us are more physically attractive than others. But what about in eternity? Will all of our bodies be raised with an equally dazzling beauty, rendering us all de facto runway models? Or will the real change come in our transformed perspective of what constitutes real beauty?

You find yourself wandering among the cool stone walls and silently flickering candles of the great Ovieto Cathedral. As you take in the stillness, you make your way over to the adjoining Chapel of the Madonna di San Brizio. There in the chapel you see a dramatic painting on the fresco above—Luis Signorelli's five-century-old masterpiece, "Resurrection of the Flesh."

The famous painting, completed by the artist in 1501, is an unforgettable work that reveals Signorelli's masterful ability to depict the human form in various poses. The biblical inspiration behind the impressive image is the vivid valley of dry bones described in Ezekiel 37:7–10:

> So I prophesied as I was commanded. And as I was prophesying, there was a noise, a rattling sound, and the bones came together, bone to bone. I looked, and tendons and flesh appeared on them and skin covered them, but there was no breath in them.
>
> Then he said to me, "Prophesy to the breath; prophesy, son of man, and say to it, 'This is what the Sovereign LORD says: Come, breath,

from the four winds and breathe into these slain, that they may live.'"
So I prophesied as he commanded me, and breath entered them; they
came to life and stood up on their feet—a vast army.

Signorelli captures the scene with striking force as he depicts individuals in various stages of resurrection, ranging from shifting jumbles of
bones to living, breathing, fully enfleshed people.

The Problem with *Resurrection of the Flesh*

Despite the impressive nature of the image, there is an interesting
problem with it. Take a good look. What do you think it is?

Contrary to those with Victorian sensibilities, the problem is *not*
that all the resurrected figures are blushingly naked (not a fig leaf in
sight). After all, Ezekiel 37 makes no mention of those resurrected
being clothed. Nor is the problem that people are resurrected as men
and women. Yet this does seem to be a concern for the many people
who believe (as I once did) that human beings will be resurrected
into some sort of asexual, quasi-angelic existence. That "angelic"
view continues to exert a wide influence. I see it firsthand every year
when I teach the doctrine of the resurrection to seminarians; some
students always object to the notion that our resurrected bodies will
be gendered. Those concerns are typically supported with an appeal
to Matthew 22:30, the passage where Jesus states that resurrected
people "will neither marry nor be given in marriage; they will be like
the angels in heaven." Based on this passage, some students conclude
that human beings will be resurrected genderless, just like the angels.

But that's *not* what Jesus says. The point he is making is not that
resurrected humans will be nongendered beings like angels. Rather,
he's simply pointing out that people, like angels, will not participate in
marriage. To read into the text that they will not be married *because*
they will be rendered genderless is simply not warranted.[1]

The problem with Signorelli's depiction of the resurrection is neither that the people are naked nor that they are gendered. The *real*
problem, I submit, is with the homogeneity of Signorelli's resurrection
portrayal: in short, *everybody looks the same.*

The ethnic homogeneity of the image is obvious. Given that Signorelli was aiming for a picture of the *general* resurrection, it should be
of some concern to us that all the people resurrected look like they
came from Western Europe.

For our purposes I'm going to focus on another aspect of the homogeneity: namely, the limited range of *body types* represented in the image. Signorelli includes no short and squat individuals, none that are tall and skinny, none that are bald or have oversized ears or disproportionately long arms or short legs. Indeed, each of the men looks like a member of the US Olympic power-lifting team. Apparently Signorelli's vision of a perfected masculinity means being built like Michelangelo's David, with a touch of Hercules for good measure. And the few women visible conform closely to the buxom Renaissance ideal of femininity famously depicted in Botticelli's Venus. This is not exactly a representative cross section of human diversity.

Signorelli's ideal may appeal to a fourteen-year-old boy who dreams of looking like Arnold Schwarzenegger in his *Conan the Barbarian* prime. But many men have no desire to look like the muscle-bound Austrian. Signorelli clearly assumed that all resurrected persons will conform to one particular standard of physical attractiveness and perfection.

Is Beauty Culturally Relative?

We need to recognize what Signorelli did not, namely that his *God's Gym* depiction of the resurrection was formed and informed by his cultural norms and individual preferences. Naomi Wolf makes the point in her modern feminist classic *The Beauty Myth* when she observes, "'Beauty' is not universal or changeless, though the West pretends that all ideals of female beauty stem from one Platonic Ideal Woman."[2] Whatever one's standards may be—Michelangelo's David and Botticelli's Venus, or Brad Pitt and Angelina Jolie—they are not simply dropped from the clouds like perfect, platonic ideals. Standards of attractiveness are formed in the thickness of human culture and personal preference.

Sociological studies provide ample data to corroborate the fact that culture shapes perceptions of physical attractiveness. For example, sociologist Jennifer O'Dea observes that a survey of Australian school children on weight perception revealed that more than one-third of obese girls of Aboriginal, Pacific Islander, and Southern European background viewed their excessive weight neutrally or even positively. This perspective, however, was "glaringly absent" among young obese girls of Anglo/Caucasian and Asian ethnicity. O'Dea argues that the difference in self-perception traces to socialization and cultural background as "a way of holding on to their cultural identity in spite of the western cultural ideal of being slim."[3]

In order to find the social forces that shape perceptions of beauty, we need look no further than the rapidly evolving standards of female attractiveness in the modern West. While Marilyn Monroe was considered an archetype of femininity in the early sixties, by the end of the decade her body type was viewed as a *plus size* in contrast to the waif-thin Twiggy and her many imitators. Like the fickle, changing fashions of skirt length and tie width, so changes the fashion of attractive body type.

Many cultures prize girth as attractive in the male form. While Signorelli may have accurately represented Renaissance European cultural standards of masculinity, a Japanese depiction of resurrection perfection may well look for inspiration to barrel-chested Taiho Koki, the greatest sumo wrestler in the last sixty years.

The culturally framed way that we perceive beauty forces us to ask whether there are *any* universal forms of beauty. In ancient Greek literature, the most beautiful of all women was Helen of Troy. In his classic play *Doctor Faustus*, Christopher Marlowe famously refers to Helen as the "face that launch'd a thousand ships." But would Helen launch a thousand ships today? Or are our standards of beauty so different from the ancient Greeks' that Helen would only be good enough for a couple rowboats?

One way to answer this question is by considering an extreme and uncontroversial case of physical ugliness, and to take that case as objective evidence that beauty is not completely in the eye of the beholder. With that in mind, I nominate poor Joseph Carey Merrick (ignominiously known as the Elephant Man) to the task. Merrick grew up in England in the late nineteenth century and was afflicted by an ailment that many scientists now believe was a combination of neurofibromatosis type 1 and Proteus syndrome. Merrick was profoundly disfigured by his pathology, and he suffered tremendously as a result, as much from the social marginalization as from the ailments themselves. Looking at Merrick's tragically disfigured form—the huge tumor on his head, his disfigured claw hand—it is clearly absurd to claim that beauty is wholly in the eye of the beholder. Merrick's body was not formed the way it was supposed to be, and as a result he was physically ugly.

The challenge is to retain the claim that there is objective ugliness and, by implication, objective beauty, while also recognizing that our perceptions of beauty are culturally formed. Can we affirm both? Indeed, we find the balance by affirming both that there are many distinct exemplifications of objective beauty and that our cultural formation and personal preference can lead us to prefer one of these exemplifications rather than another. In this way we can affirm that Michelangelo's David and sumo wrestler Taiho Koki may represent distinct and fully compatible ideal exemplifications of the male form, but Joseph Merrick does not.

Will We All Be Equally Beautiful?

Now that we've recognized that people can be objectively more or less beautiful, we can turn to the next question: Will all resurrected people be equally objectively attractive, or will some be more attractive than others?

One thing is beyond dispute: people will be more physically attractive when they're resurrected than they are now. An extreme case like that of Joseph Merrick provides an obvious example. Assuming Merrick is raised to eternal life, we may not know how he will look at the resurrection, but we can surely have a good idea how he will *not* look. Gone will be the grotesque tumors and disfigurements that marred his body during his short and painful life when he is brought into resurrection life anew.

But if God will heal Merrick's ugly deformities, what will he do for less extreme deviations from the standards of beauty? Virtually all of us fail to exemplify perfectly a form of beauty. Does that mean that God will give each of us a makeover to ensure that our resurrected bodies conform perfectly to some idealized form? Will he shorten disproportionately long arms? Trim the excessively bushy unibrow? Grow the stubby legs? Dissolve excess body fat? Enliven and tame that impossibly frizzy hair? Provide collagen injections for thin lips?

It seems perfectly right to affirm that God will heal Merrick's body and in doing so will render it more beautiful. Just as long as we don't end up at the top of a slippery slope in which any deviation from a particular standard of beauty, however trivial, must be corrected. Once we take that position, God begins to look less like the Great Physician and more like a glorified cosmetic surgeon, nipping and tucking the whole lot of us until we all conform to one or another standard of beauty.

Jesus, Beautifully Plain, and Plainly Beautiful

At this point I think we can make some headway by considering the resurrection body of Jesus. Was he physically beautiful in his life on earth? If not, is there evidence that he became more beautiful at the resurrection?

Let's start with the first question. The one place where we find a comment on the physical attractiveness of Jesus is in Isaiah 53:2 (a messianic, Suffering-Servant passage) where we read: "He had no beauty or majesty to attract us to him, nothing in his appearance that we should desire him." Many Christian theologians have argued from this passage that Jesus was physically unattractive. For example, Tertullian refers to the "ignoble appearance" of Jesus and observes, "His body did not reach even to human beauty, to say nothing of heavenly glory."[4] The idea is not that Jesus was unusually ugly, just that he was rather plain.

There is nothing elsewhere in Scripture to contradict Isaiah's testimony. Indeed, the general silence on Jesus's physical appearance in the New Testament and early church supports the conclusion that he was not notably handsome or ugly.

If Jesus was rather plain, is it possible that at the resurrection he was physically transformed into a striking human specimen? So far as I can see, the best biblical prospect for defending this hypothesis is rooted in the failure of people to recognize the resurrected Jesus when they first see him. There are several notable examples of recognition failure, including Mary at the tomb (John 20:11–16), the apostles fishing (John 21:4), and the disciples on the road to Emmaus (Luke 24:13–35). Thus, one could conclude that the disciples failed to recognize Jesus in the same way that a socialite in Boca Raton may fail to recognize her friend at Starbucks after her latest cosmetic surgery.

It's an interesting hypothesis, but alas, there are several critical problems with it. To begin with, there are far better, and simpler, explanations for the failure of people to recognize Jesus. To begin with, nobody was *expecting* to see Jesus, so it is little surprise that they didn't immediately recognize him. Further details serve to explain the specifics of each case. For example, Mary's case can be explained by the fact that she initially didn't get a direct view of Jesus in the early morning light of the garden. But as soon as Jesus looked directly at her, she recognized him immediately (John 20:16). Something similar could explain the failure of the apostles to recognize Jesus standing on the shore. As for the disciples on the road to Emmaus, the text explicitly says that they were *kept* from recognizing him (Luke 24:16). This suggests that in this case at least, supernatural, divine intervention, rather than newly acquired good looks, was the reason for the failure of recognition.

The second problem with the hypothesis is that when people did realize it was Jesus, they didn't attribute their initial perception failure to Jesus's new attractiveness. Mary didn't report to the disciples, "I have seen the Lord . . . and wow, is he handsome!" She simply reported matter-of-factly that she'd seen the Lord (John 20:18). When he finally recognizes Jesus standing on the shore, John exclaims, "It is the Lord!" (John 21:7) Similarly, the men on the road to Emmaus never say they failed to recognize Jesus because he had become so good-looking (Luke 24:32). Nor does Thomas exclaim that Jesus had become handsome. Instead, he simply corroborates the wounds (John 20:27–28).

At this point, a person determined to affirm that Jesus must be eternally beautiful could always retreat to the claim that he became physically beautiful still later at the ascension. The problem with that claim is that it is hopelessly ad hoc, and there is no independent evidence to support it.[5]

This leads us to the most likely conclusion that Jesus's body was physically plain during his life and remained physically plain in the resurrection. If there are archetypes of male attractiveness, it appears that he does not exemplify one of them. Is this a problem?

Does It Matter if Jesus Was Plain?

I don't think it matters if Jesus was not handsome. On the contrary, I think this fact challenges us to recognize that physical beauty may not be as important as our cultural and personal fixations suggest. Consider the case of Cleopatra. While this great Egyptian princess has been famed for centuries as an archetype of female attractiveness, the evidence suggests that she was not conventionally beautiful. (On this point she has often been contrasted with Queen Nefertiti, who has been lauded as an exemplar of a classic form of beauty.) Indeed, Cleopatra was described by her contemporaries as having a dispro-portionately large mouth and hooked nose. As Plutarch delicately put it, "Her beauty, we are told, was in itself not altogether incomparable, nor such as to strike those who saw her."[6]

If Cleopatra wasn't physically attractive, what was it that led people to recognize her as beautiful? Plutarch explains the real nature of her attractiveness:

Converse with her had an irresistible charm, and her presence, combined with the persuasiveness of her discourse and the character which was somehow diffused about her behavior toward others, had something stimulating about it. There was sweetness also in the tones of her voice; and her tongue, like an instrument of many strings, she could readily turn to whatever language she pleased.[7]

In short, people found Cleopatra attractive not simply because she conformed to a physical standard of beauty but because she had an alluring, charismatic, and winsome character.

If Cleopatra could draw people to herself by the force of her character, how much more attractive will we find the incarnate Son of God? Even if Jesus does not conform to conventional standards of beauty, that will hardly matter for anyone who knows him. He will still be, to borrow a line from the hymn "Lily of the Valley," the "fairest of ten thousand to my soul."[8]

If Jesus is so glorious that we are irresistibly drawn to his presence, then when we are fully conformed to his image, we too will exemplify a greater attractiveness than can be imagined now. Even if the degree of physical beauty of our resurrection bodies will vary, as I suspect it will, such differences will be negligible relative to the profound allure we will all exert as fully sanctified sons and daughters made in and restored to the image of God that is Jesus Christ.

Heavenly Questions

1. Do you think Jesus was physically plain or handsome? Does it matter?

2. Do you think there are objective standards of beauty, or do you think beauty is wholly relative to cultural or personal preference?

3. How would you like your resurrection body to differ from the present form of your body?

Question 8

Will Anyone Be Deaf?

Creation is full of sounds, from the chirp of crickets to the cascade of a waterfall, from the lonely call of the loon to the soothing rustle of the leaves. I suspect that such sounds capture something of what the psalmist meant by declaring that creation pours forth speech (Ps. 19:2). But what about those who cannot hear this speech? What about those who cannot hear at all? Will they be able to hear in heaven—even if they don't want to?

When John the Baptist found himself wrestling with doubts about whether Jesus was the Messiah, Jesus responded by pointing to the signs of his work, including healing the deaf (Matt. 11:5; Luke 7:22; cf. Mark 7:31–37).[1] This made perfect sense since the Israelites believed that miraculous healing provided a sign of the coming of God's kingdom.

It seems that the meaning of the sign couldn't be more straightforward: When God's kingdom comes, and his will is done on earth as it is in heaven, then the blind shall see, the lame shall walk, and the deaf will all hear.

But what if some people don't *want* to hear?

It is difficult for those who are hearing to conceive of those who are deaf being perfectly content with their situation. It is even more difficult for us to conceive that they *ought* to be perfectly content.

When most people think of deafness, they *only* think of a disability, an auditory deficiency. It's at that point that we've already been led astray, for deafness is about much more than being unable to hear. Those who write on the topic distinguish between the condition of auditory deprivation that they call being "deaf," and identity with a community of people who share a common culture and sign language—for example, ASL (American Sign Language)—that they call being "Deaf."[2]

Once we have that distinction in place, we can see that the issue is not merely about *deafness*—an auditory deprivation—but about *Deafness*—a cultural identity. And we can begin to appreciate that the well-intentioned claim that all deaf people should be healed of their auditory deficiency can begin to sound like a subversively imperialistic claim that all Deaf people should be "healed" of their cultural identity.

Carol Padden and Tom Humphries point out that there are many distinct Deaf cultures in the world.[3] The first modern Deaf culture arose in France with the founding of the first school for deaf children in 1761. A community developed around this school and with it a form of sign language. American Sign Language, which grew out of this early French sign language, is itself an independent language of signs that contrasts with spoken and written English at several points, including its rich verb morphology and sentence structure. Padden and Humphries observe, "The mistaken belief that ASL is a set of simple gestures with no internal structure has led to the tragic misconception that the relationship of Deaf people to their sign language is a casual one that can be easily severed and replaced." The substantial populations of Deaf communities and their established patterns of cultural transmission and shared languages together constitute a rich culture.[4]

Deaf in *Sound and Fury*

Is it possible to advocate for the healing of deafness without incautiously proposing the elimination of Deafness? For those of us who are not Deaf and thus have a difficult time envisioning what it means to be a part of this vibrant culture, the complex issues are helpfully illumined in the fascinating Academy Award–nominated documentary *Sound and Fury.*[5] The film tells the story of two families facing the complexities of being deaf (and Deaf) in the world of the hearing. One family is entirely deaf and is composed of Peter and Nita Artinian and their daughter, Heather. Both Peter and Nita are content with being deaf. In the film Peter signs:

> I would never say I prefer to be hearing. I really am happy being deaf. It's very peaceful. Who would want to change that? In my heart I know this is who I am. If somebody gave me a pill that made me hearing, would I take it? No way. I'd want to go to a hospital and throw it up and go back to being deaf. *I want to be deaf.*

This is where things get complicated. Peter and Nita's five-year-old daughter, Heather, is *not* happy about being deaf. She has begun asking her parents for a cochlear implant, which would allow her to be hearing like her friends. But her parents are resistant because they worry that once the world of the hearing is opened to her, she will lose her Deaf culture and the close ties that bind it together. Nita observes that while she understands her daughter's desire to hear, ultimately she wants young Heather to be happy the way she is.

At one point in the film Nita is sitting at the kitchen table with her sister-in-law Mary who, though hearing, was raised by deaf parents and has a deaf child herself. Consequently, Mary understands much of Deaf culture even though she can hear. Nita tells Mary of her resistance to the cochlear implant and her fear that it will undermine Deaf culture.

This is too much for Mary, who retorts incredulously, "Why is it so important to be Deaf? Yes, Deaf people have a beautiful language, but you miss out on so many other beautiful things in the world, like music."

Nita signs back in frustration, "I don't care about music! *I can't hear it!*"

As the chasm between the two looms, Mary struggles to express to Nita all that she is missing by being unable to hear: "It's hearing a baby cry for the first time or being outside and hearing the beautiful rain. You can hear the rain falling on the ground."

But Nita is unmoved: "Mary, you don't understand. Wait a minute. You are hearing. You can hear. I never hear. For me this is normal. I can see the beautiful rain. I can taste the rain on my lips. It doesn't matter to me to hear it. It makes no sense to me."

Mary protests: "But Nita, you never experienced hearing. *I know* what you're missing."

Therein lies the dilemma. Can Mary really understand what Nita could lose by hearing? Can Nita possibly understand what she would gain? Can either truly make a fully informed decision on the matter?

Deaf in Heaven?

Since all the best diversity on earth reflects something of God's own being—and there is much good in Deaf culture—some theologians have proposed that God can be meaningfully described as Deaf.[6] While some Deaf liberation theologians have gone so far as to say that God is physically deaf, Wayne Morris argues more plausibly that God is culturally Deaf: "If it is the case that when all people are in community together that they can then claim to be made in the image of God, there must be some aspect of God that is Deaf, as well as hearing, sighted, blind, old, young, black, white, male and female."[7] If the best of human experience is rooted in God's being, then surely Deaf culture is an expression of the goodness of God as surely as hearing culture.

So how do we bring this culture into heaven? If we don't want to lose the best of Deaf culture, perhaps we can argue that in heaven all people will be able to hear, but they will also appreciate and be able to participate in Deaf culture. This seems to be a reasonable solution. After all, Mary seems to understand Deaf culture even though she herself can hear. Perhaps one day we will all be able to hear even as we can also understand and even participate in Deaf culture.

A more radical solution would propose that some people could choose to have a deaf resurrection body for the sake of maintaining their Deaf culture in heaven. If people like Peter Artinian are content to be deaf, if they find it peaceful and positive, then should they be given the ability to hear even if they would prefer not to have it? Perhaps part of the rich diversity of heaven will encompass communities of people who choose to live eternally in the fertile soil of peaceful silence that they have come to love. Ought we to offer healing to "disabled" persons who have embraced their identity and enriched their communities as a result and who no longer want the healing offered?

Heavenly Questions

1. Some Deaf people argue that their inability to hear is actually a blessing from God because it has made available to them a culture and experience of reality that they would not exercise otherwise. What do you think?

2. Do you think the heavenly community will include any bodies
   with disabilities? What is a disability anyway?

3. Do you think the church is sensitive to the needs of minority
   communities with disabilities? If not, how can it become more
   sensitive?

Question 9

Will We Still Get Thirsty, Hungry, and Sleepy?

It is commonly assumed that in heaven all our needs will be met and all our desires will finally be satisfied. But some of the greatest pleasures of life come as a result of satiating unsatisfied drives. A drink that quenches great thirst, a meal that quells intense hunger, and a rest following a period of deep exhaustion are all that much sweeter because of the contrasting state of want that preceded them. Will heaven allow the experience of such deprivations for the added pleasure of satisfying them?

In the mid-1990s I took a road trip in the height of summer through the desert in the Southwest. In one long day I drove across New Mexico and Arizona on I-40 and then up Highway 93 into Nevada. Despite the triple-digit temperatures, for some inexplicable reason I had resolved not to use the air conditioning, choosing instead to brave the torrid summer heat with the windows rolled down.

After several hours of being buffeted by the scorching desert winds, I finally arrived in Las Vegas in the early evening, exhausted, dehydrated, and (given that I hadn't had a sip to drink since Winslow) completely parched.

I parked the car, walked across a vast parking lot with heat radiating off the pavement, and went into a casino. Immediately I was enveloped by the deliciously cool air. What a breathtaking contrast with the blasting heat to which I'd subjected myself for hours in my drive across Arizona. Never had air conditioning felt so good. I made a beeline for the bar, sat down, and ordered a Coke. The drink arrived chilled and frosty in my hot and dusty hand. Cool beads of condensation rolled down the outside of the glass, creating inviting little rivulets of refreshment. As I grabbed the beverage, the ice sparkled and shifted in the bubbly dark liquid. Then I placed the straw to my lips and began to slurp the drink, and in the ensuing euphoric moments, I brushed against sensory transcendence.

Life's Great Pleasures

Had I spent the afternoon lounging in the air-conditioned lobby of the casino prior to ordering the Coke, I would have remembered neither the cool air nor the ice-cold drink. But I *hadn't* spent the afternoon in the air-conditioned casino. I'd been travelling through a scorching desert bereft of refreshment. For that reason, I still remember intimately the details of that experience twenty years later. The deprivation I experienced in the desert during my long drive—the dryness, the heat, the dust, the thirst—enriched immeasurably my subsequent experience of the air conditioning and the cold soft drink.

This phenomenon of intensified pleasure following deprivation is an example of the contrast effect—the psychological effect according to which our perception of a present state is altered (positively or negatively) by the contrast with another closely proximate state. To give one simple example, "A $70 sweater may not seem like a very good deal initially, but if you learn that the sweater was reduced from $200, all of a sudden it may seem like a real bargain."[1] There is nothing like regular list price to make the discount appear to be a great deal. And there's nothing like searing desert heat to make air conditioning and a cool drink positively delicious.

The contrast effect is clearly operative where our bodily drives are concerned. We are all familiar with the fact that periods of sensory deprivation can greatly intensify the pleasure when that drive is satisfied. Martin Luther ably describes the contrast effect with an old German saying: "To them, as the proverb saith, 'hunger is the best sauce': that hunger, renders this food wonderfully savory."[2] No doubt we can all remember times when we ate after being famished. There is nothing so delicious as a well-prepared meal following a period of great hunger.

This principle is not limited to food and drink. Consider another one of life's great pleasures: sleep. In this case the deprivation consists of exhaustion, the desire to find rest. Consequently, when rest finally comes, it is a heady delight. The opening of the book *The Sleep Instinct* eloquently describes this great pleasure of life:

> Like a great river flowing through a city, the sleep instinct flows gently but powerfully through our lives. While we can do nothing to stem its flow, we can and do come to terms with this natural force by sacrificing to it one whole third of our life. Indeed our sacrifice is often an enthusiastic one and sleep is rated by many as one of the greatest pleasures of life. They look forward to bedtime and savor the hours spent in bed until they reluctantly get up in the morning.[3]

I recall one particular day when I had been driving on the road for hours. During the long, ponderous drive I became so drowsy that I resorted to playing the stereo as loud as it would go and slapping myself periodically on the cheeks just to keep myself awake. After I finally arrived home and enjoyed warm family greetings and a quick meal, at long last I made my way to the bed with an irrepressible giddiness in anticipation of the imminent promise of sleep. As I laid my weary head down, I joyfully pushed off with abandon from the shores of wakefulness and was blissfully carried away by the great, flowing river of slumber.

Thirsty, Hungry, and Sleepy in Heaven?

As we contemplate how sensory pleasures like drinking, eating, and sleeping are intensified when they follow a period of deprivation, we find ourselves facing a dilemma. On the one hand, heaven promises to be the summation of all the greatest pleasures, and thus it should include the greatest of sensory experiences. Yet on the other hand, the perfection of heaven seems to preclude the suffering from want—including thirst, hunger, and exhaustion—that these experiences require. Given that John promises a heaven in which the old order of things will have passed away (Rev. 21:4), how can we still experience the thirst, hunger, and exhaustion that typify that old order?

We can illustrate the dilemma as follows: Let's say that you desire to have the greenest and cleanest lawn in your neighborhood. You then discover, however, that the secret to having the greenest lawn is spreading fresh cow manure. This presents you with a dilemma, for if you spread the manure, you may have the *greenest* lawn, but you will not have the *cleanest* lawn. Consequently, you are forced to choose whether your lawn will be green or clean.

Just as the greenest lawn requires at least some manure, so the most pleasurable experiences of drink, food, and sleep require at least some degree of the contrasting states of thirst, hunger, and exhaustion. Given this fact, could it be that the promise of every tear being wiped away is consistent with the occasional parched throat, hunger pang, and deep yawn?

In the case of the lawn, it seems to me that the best way out of the dilemma is to bite the bullet and realize that the best lawn in the neighborhood will be neither the greenest nor the cleanest. Rather, it will represent the *optimal balance* between the values of being clean and being green, meaning just the right amount of manure without excessively soiling the grass.

The same type of reasoning applies to our present conundrum. At some point the suffering experienced as a result of thirst, hunger, or exhaustion would be so intense that the added pleasure that accompanies eventual satiation would be insufficient to outweigh it. God knows where this point is and will ensure that in heaven we never suffer more than is required to achieve the maximum pleasure-enriching contrast effect.

An Equation of Pleasure

We can illustrate this idea by ascribing some arbitrary numerical values to degrees of pleasure and suffering in a simplified comparison of three possible scenarios. In each case, pleasure is granted a positive pleasure score, suffering is given a negative pleasure score, while lack of pleasure or suffering yields a neutral pleasure score of zero. Then all these scores are added to arrive at the cumulative pleasure score (CPS). The higher the CPS, the more likely God will actualize that scenario in heaven.

We begin with scenario 1:

1. never experiencing thirst (0) + never experiencing the satisfaction of satiating thirst (0) = 0 (CPS)

In scenario 1, we never suffer from thirst, but neither do we experience the pleasure that comes with satisfying thirst. This yields a CPS of 0, and it constitutes the neutral, baseline position.

Next we consider scenario 2—the first of two possibilities that involve allowing some limited suffering (e.g., thirst, hunger, and exhaustion) in order to intensify the pleasure that can be experienced as a result:

2. experiencing extreme thirst (–10) + experiencing the satisfaction of satiating extreme thirst (8) = –2 CPS

In this second scenario, the cumulative loss that results from the suffering induced by extreme thirst is so great that it overwhelms the pleasure experienced by the eventual slaking of that thirst. Given that the pleasure suffers a net loss over suffering, and thus the person is worse off than he or she would have been if never thirsty, God would have an overriding reason not to actualize scenario 2.

This brings us to our third scenario in which the suffering from thirst is reduced but not eliminated altogether:

3. experiencing modest thirst (–5) + experiencing the satisfaction of modest thirst (7) = 2 CPS

In this third possibility, the suffering from thirst is significantly reduced while the satisfaction from the satiation of thirst is only modestly reduced. This result is a CPS of 2—a score that exceeds both the first and second scenarios. Consequently, all things being equal, God has reason to actualize scenario 3 given that it presents a higher CPS score and thus an optimal balance of pleasure over suffering. This thought experiment allows us to see how the satisfaction of various drives like thirst, hunger, and exhaustion could conceivably be experienced in heaven to the degree that doing so would intensify our cumulative pleasure.

At first blush this conclusion seems to place us in tension with the biblical images that describe heaven as a satisfaction of drives. For example, one of the central symbols for the new creation is the banquet. As we read in Isaiah 25:6:

On this mountain the LORD Almighty will prepare
a feast of rich food for all peoples,

a banquet of aged wine—
the best of meats and the finest of wines.

This image presents satisfaction from want, not the ongoing experience of thirst and hunger (see also Rev. 19:9). Or consider another common symbol of the new kingdom—the Sabbath rest. We read in Hebrews 4:9–11:

There remains, then, a Sabbath-rest for the people of God; for anyone who enters God's rest also rests from their works, just as God did from his. Let us, therefore, make every effort to enter that rest, so that no one will perish by following their example of disobedience.

This too makes no mention of ongoing exhaustion for the intensification of rest. In all these cases, the ongoing deprivation appears to be limited to this present age with satisfaction occurring in the next age. So isn't this discussion misguided?

The problem with that kind of response is that it interprets these symbolic images much too woodenly. Imagine that an American couple adopts a half-starved child named Andrei from Romania. When they bring him home they promise him, "Andrei, you will never want for food again." Four months later on Thanksgiving, Andrei is sitting in the living room smelling the intoxicating aroma of turkey, mashed potatoes, and gravy being prepared in the kitchen. He is so hungry that he is barely able to contain his anticipation. Have Andrei's new parents broken their promise by allowing him to develop an appetite waiting for the turkey dinner? Of course not. The promise of Andrei's parents is concerned with the suffering from a systemic lack of food, not the anticipation of a delicious meal. The biblical promises of Sabbath rest and culinary satisfaction should be viewed similarly in that they do not preclude the ongoing experience of sensory deprivations that hold the imminent promise of being fulfilled.

The Pleasures of Modest Suffering

In closing, I want to revisit our third scenario. According to this calculation, the experience of modest thirst was arbitrarily demarcated to be −5. But there are two good reasons to believe that this displeasure in heaven will not be as bad as we may first think.

To begin with, the anticipation of the satisfaction of a drive can provide a satisfaction all its own that can ameliorate the suffering endured during the period of denial. Imagine, for example, that you are fasting and plan to break your fast with a delicious meal at 9:00 p.m. The anticipation of the meal throughout the day provides an anticipatory pleasure that ameliorates the suffering of the fast. When I was driving across Arizona, the anticipation of a cold drink in Las Vegas sustained me in this way. By contrast, if I had experienced that same level of thirst while stranded in the desert with no imminent promise of drink, the same experience of thirst would be much worse given the level of psychological fear and uncertainty accompanying the experience.

Second, the experience of suffering can, in certain cases, bring additional pleasure that is rooted in the way it opens one to a vitality of experience. Why else do people go through the insanity of participating in a polar bear plunge in which they jump into a frozen lake in the middle of winter? The invigorating experience of jumping into icy water is not pleasurable in itself, but it does facilitate a vital and memorable experience along with a sense of accomplishment that is, on balance, pleasurable—at least for some people. The same reasoning can keep a person running a marathon, climbing a mountain, or in my case, driving through Arizona in the summer without using the air conditioning.

All this is to say that even if the cumulative suffering of an experience of hunger, thirst, or exhaustion were −5, there is good reason to believe that the cumulative pleasures derived from both the experience and its satisfaction would far outweigh that comparatively trivial suffering. And for these reasons we should expect that we will still experience some hunger, thirst, and exhaustion in heaven.

HEAVENLY QUESTIONS

1. Do you agree that the experience of thirst, hunger, and exhaustion can intensify pleasure? Can you think of any experiences of your own in which this was true?

2. Can you imagine enjoying a meal without experiencing any hunger as the motivation for eating?

3. Do you think we will sleep in heaven? Why or why not?

Question 10

Will There Be Sweet Melancholy?

Poets have long been fascinated with the concept of sweet melancholy—a state of emotional satisfaction in limited emotional suffering. Does the promise of every tear being wiped from our eyes exclude the place for sweet melancholy in our resurrected emotional life?

The promise of Revelation 21:4 that every tear will be wiped away surely encompasses deliverance from mourning and sadness. As Jesus promises in the second Beatitude, "Blessed are those who mourn, for they will be comforted" (Matt. 5:4). This is great news for Christians who have struggled with deep sadness and depression. Emotional pain can be devastating. Sally Brampton recalls one of her friends describing his depression: "'Dying,' he recalled, 'feels like nothing against the fear of going through another episode of severe depression. I don't think I could do it again.'"[1] In light of these kinds of experiences, it may seem rather bizarre to suggest that any sense of melancholy—any enduring sadness—will continue in heaven.

On Sweet Melancholy

To be sure, we can all agree that there is no room in eternity for debilitating melancholy of the kind described by Sally Brampton's friend. Such extreme and unrewarding suffering will indeed be part of the old order that will pass away. But this doesn't necessarily mean that there will be no melancholy at all. Just as there may be room for the drives of hunger and thirst that enrich the banquet, could there also be room for a dimension of melancholy to the extent that it could enrich our emotional life in eternity? Of course that possibility depends on whether there can be a melancholy that enriches our emotional life and thus can meaningfully be called *sweet*.

The idea of sweet melancholy appears in popular seventies pop singer Burton Cummings's song "Timeless Love," in which the singer croons that even missing his beloved feels good. At first blush this may seem nonsensical. How can it possibly feel good to *miss* someone you love? How can there be pleasure in the unsatisfied drive for physical intimacy? Counterintuitive though it may seem, the concept of sweet melancholy that the song assumes is one well familiar to philosophers and poets who recognize the value in an enriched emotional life that is made possible by some emotional deprivation.

Let's begin with the general observation that many things that are very healthy in small amounts become toxic in larger amounts. Consider some gastronomic examples. Potatoes are a delicious and nutritious food in moderate doses, but they contain glycoalkaloids, which are toxic when taken in excess. The same is true of almonds. While they are very healthy in moderate doses, the small amount of hydrogen cyanide in almonds can become poisonous when they are eaten in a large amount. Life is full of such examples.

I propose thinking of melancholy as analogous to potatoes and almonds—nutritious in moderate doses but poisonous if taken to excess. If this is true, then just as a well-rounded physical diet can be enriched by a moderate amount of potatoes and almonds, so a well-rounded emotional diet can be enriched by a moderate amount of melancholy.

Sweet Melancholy and True Sadness

As I said, poets are well familiar with sweet melancholy. One of the most poetic descriptions I've discovered is found in Mary Hays's

eighteenth-century novel *Memoirs of Emma Courtney*. In the words
of the protagonist, Emma:

> The sweet melancholy which I defend is never sad; it is only a modifica-
> tion of pleasure from which it borrows all its charms. Like those gilded
> clouds embellished by a setting sun, the light vapours of melancholy
> intercept the rays of pleasure, and present them under a new and
> agreeable aspect. It is a delicious balm for the wounds of the heart; it
> is a salutary alloy to the vivacity of joy; attempered by it, that passion
> is rendered more impressive and more lasting.[2]

According to this description, melancholy is a conduit for the experience of pleasure as are the vapors that convey the rays of the sun.
While this is a helpful description, the strength of this passage is
found more in its poetic cadence than its propositional clarity. You
still may be thinking, if sweet melancholy is "never sad," then why
call it melancholy at all? Isn't that just a confusion of terms?

Romanian philosopher Emile M. Cioran was familiar with the
experience of melancholy in his own life and writings. Known for his
intense, lyrical approach to philosophy and a pessimism that char-
acterized his philosophical output, he shows a unique perspective
on the value of limited emotional suffering. Cioran contrasts sweet
melancholy with true sadness at several points.

To begin with, sweet melancholy (which he refers to simply as
"melancholy") includes hope: "At the end of all melancholy there is
a chance of consolation or resignation. Its esthetic aspect holds possibilities for future harmony that are absent from profound organic
sadness. The latter ends in the irrevocable, the former in graceful
dream."[3] The presence of hope allows for sweet melancholy to be
framed by the pleasure that arises with the anticipation of relief and
fulfillment, much like the physical drives we analyzed in the previous chapter. Cioran writes: "That one can never speak of a funeral
as 'melancholy' shows an important difference between sadness and
melancholy."[4]

Second, sweet melancholy possesses an aesthetic dimension absent
from general sadness.[5] Like a piece of dark chocolate that has just
the right balance of bitterness and sweetness to enliven the cocoa and
provide a tasty confection, so sweet melancholy provides just enough
bitterness and sweetness to enrich the aesthetic dimension of one's
emotional life.

Finally, sweet melancholy lacks the emotional intensity present in sadness. Cioran describes this aspect as calmness. While deep sadness is domineering and debilitating, sweet melancholy is more a subtle echo that serves to enrich and enliven like Emma Courtney's vapors that mediate the sun's rays. This calmness can be manifested in various ways. For example, Cioran points to regret: "Though regret may be persistent, it is never so intense as to cause deep suffering. Regret expresses affectively a profound phenomenon: the advance through life into death."[6]

Cioran's analysis raises many questions when set against the backdrop of eternity. For example, could the sweet melancholy of heaven involve regret? This seems doubtful to me. But it certainly could include all sorts of other aspects evident in our present experience. For instance, in the vastness of heaven you may not see a beloved friend for years, and the experience of his or her absence until you meet again may bring with it a sweet melancholy not unlike the sentiment expressed in the song by Burton Cummings.

It is also possible that sweet melancholy may lack a positive object altogether. James W. Manns refers to the sweet melancholy he experiences when listening to a Chopin nocturne.[7] His experience has no clearly defined object as the source of the melancholy, and yet the emotion still works its deepening spell on his emotional universe. There is just enough of a lingering sense of sadness or loss to enrich Manns's experience of the nocturne, and this adds to the overall emotional depth and richness of the experience. If this is the case, then there may be just enough sweet melancholy in eternity, with or without a clearly identifiable object, to enrich our emotional lives and our overall experience of heaven.

HEAVENLY QUESTIONS

1. Do you think there is such a thing as a sweetly melancholic sadness? If so, do you think it could enrich your emotional life in heaven?

2. Are there any other negative emotions that include a pleasurable element?

3. Is anger ever pleasurable? Could there be anger in heaven?

Part 3

Exploring the
Perfect Earthiness of Heaven

In this section we turn our focus from resurrected persons to the resurrected world as we see the magic of H = ep extended to other living creatures and the products of culture. Do we have the imagination to grasp the plans that God has for creation?

Question 11

Will the *Titanic* Sail Again?

The central image of the new creation is a city: the New Jerusalem. Given that a city is a complex nexus of human culture, this image suggests a sweeping redemption of human culture. But given that culture and technology have changed in unimaginable ways over millennia, we have to ask what it will mean for the cultural relics of human history to be redeemed in eternity.

While the city of Tarshish is mentioned almost two dozen times in Scripture, there is no agreement as to which ancient city is being referred to. It could be Tartessus, a Phoenician port in Spain, or Tarsus, a city in Cilicia, or perhaps some other forgotten place.[1] While we cannot be sure where Tarshish was, we do know that it had a rich naval history and a reputation sufficient to attract Jonah when he was trying to flee from God's call to Nineveh (Jon. 1:3).

Like the city itself, the ships of Tarshish were highly distinguished in the ancient world. We get a picture of what they might have looked like in Ezekiel 27 when the prophet laments the coming demise of Tyre, a seafaring city that employed ships from Tarshish in its trade. Ezekiel describes the ships of Tyre as beautiful vessels made with timber of juniper and cedars from Lebanon, with oars formed by oaks from Bashan and decks made of cypress with ivory accents. The flowing sails and waving banners were made from fine Egyptian linen. And the ships were sailed by skilled oarsmen, sailors, and shipwrights from a number of different regions (vv. 4–9, 12, 25).

Given Tarshish's military dominance, it is not surprising that its ships came to represent the oppression of the ancient Israelites and thus that the city's demise symbolized deliverance for the Israelites. The first and fourteenth verses of Isaiah 23 refer to the ships awaiting judgment, while Psalm 48:7 describes God destroying the ships with a powerful east wind. And in his lament for Tyre, Ezekiel vividly describes the city's mighty ships being shattered by the east wind and left to sink to the bottom of the sea (Ezek. 27:26).

No doubt during their time plying the waters of the Mediterranean, more than a few ships from Tarshish faced precisely that fate, creaking and groaning in a strong storm until they broke apart and sank to the bottom of the sea. And there they were left to a watery grave to face an eternity forgotten beneath the waves.

The Resurrection of the Ships of Tarshish

Is this the final chapter for all the ships of Tarshish? Have they been wiped off the pages of history once and for all, left to rot at the bottom of the Mediterranean? Or could it be that there is a place in God's resurrected world for the greatest glories of maritime culture? Could the ships of Tarshish sail again?

This is where things begin to get interesting, for the harsh judgment described in Ezekiel 27 is not the final word on the ships of Tarshish. We find a more promising picture in Isaiah 66, a passage that paints a vivid portrait of the messianic age. The prophet states that God will send his people around the world, including to Tarshish, so that his glory may come to the nations (vv. 19–24).

Even more strikingly, in Isaiah 60:9 we read that the great ships of Tarshish will play a role in that future restoration as they are commissioned in service to the Israelites. As one commentator observes, the image is of these vessels as "vehicles for the eschatological gathering of Israel to Jerusalem."[2] The image communicates how Israel will ultimately prevail as God appropriates the best of worldly culture into his kingdom. Within this new order, foreign ships that in biblical writing so often symbolized the foreign oppression of the Israelites will become heralds of the liberation of God's people.

The fact that the ships are appropriated rather than destroyed also conveys the idea of God restoring the very best of human culture for the glory of his kingdom. Perhaps we should rethink the idea that

Ezekiel 27 represents the final word on the ships of Tarshish. From this perspective, the final word may actually come ten chapters later if we think of the valley of dry bones in Ezekiel 37 as applying to the rotting timbers lying on sea bottoms around the world. Could it be that just as the dry bones of long-dead persons will draw back together and form a living person again, so those long-decayed timbers sitting at the bottom of the Mediterranean will be gathered again to resurrect a great sailing ship?

Perhaps on that day the Spirit will draw back together the atomic fragments of timbers that rotted away millennia ago. First the surface of the sea will ripple and bubble, and then the waters will part as a great, ancient ship emerges to sail again. The ropes and ivory and ancient Egyptian masts reappear dripping with water, but soon they are snapping and billowing in the breeze as they did millennia before. As the cool waters of the Mediterranean slap the sides of the ancient, restored hull, one of the great ships of Tarshish lives again.

Is this possible? Could it be that God will restore the ships of Tarshish? Or are we merely engaged in a fanciful reading into ancient prophecy?

While the references to the ships of Tarshish are symbolic in nature, that hardly precludes the possibility that the very same ships *will* sail again. And why not? God cares about the matter that composes our bodies enough to ensure that that same matter composes our bodies when they're restored. So why wouldn't God care enough about the matter that composes the best products of human culture to see that those exact products are also restored, including the great ships of Tarshish?

A Truly Titanic Resurrection

If we consider seriously that God will restore some of the great ships from the Iron Age in which Tarshish sailed, we will likewise have to ask about the grand maritime accomplishments of other ages as well. What about the once-proud *Mary Rose*, a majestic, British warship that sailed during the Reformation era? And is there hope for the fabled *Bluenose* schooner of Nova Scotia? Could there even be the possibility of future seas for the once-mighty Nazi battleship *Bismarck*? Carrying it further, if warships are restored to eternity, what will happen to their armaments? Will the canons be converted to planters? What about the massive, sixteen-inch guns of an *Iowa*-class battleship? Will they be painted pink and decorated with laurel wreaths?

While it would be wonderful to see the great ships of bygone eras sail again, none can ignite the public imagination as surely as that great steamship that went down on its maiden voyage: the mighty *Titanic*. This is an interesting time to be contemplating the restoration of the *Titanic*. In 2012 it was announced that Australian billionaire Clive Palmer is financing a replica of the *Titanic* to be completed and ready to sail in 2016. Personally, while I have no interest in taking a cruise on a modern passenger liner, the prospect of a journey across the North Atlantic on a *Titanic* replica is an enormously enticing prospect.

It also provides a strikingly tangible picture for the restoration of creation. If an Australian billionaire can build a replica of the *Titanic*, certainly God can restore the original ship. Could it be that Palmer's replica provides a foretaste of a future time when we will not sail mere replicas? Could it be that the sediments of the North Atlantic will be churned up again, this time to release their grip on the enormous iron hull of this great ship as it is raised and restored for service in a new creation?

Some people may wonder why God would bother to bring obsolete, human cultural artifacts back again. But that kind of puzzlement fails to recognize the historical and personal significance of the products of human culture. I imagine our appreciation for the restoration of culture would be deepened if we could see the joy of a man who worked in the Dublin shipyard constructing the original *Titanic* being invited to work on the reconstruction of the mighty vessel for eternity.

The skepticism of cultural resurrection also fails to recognize that there is much more to life than greater technical efficiency. A Kindle loaded up with three thousand digital books may be more streamlined than a dusty old library with a crackling fireplace, but that hardly means that the former can replace the latter without loss. Heaven will surely have room for the Kindle, but might it have room for the library as well?

This leaves me with a high degree of confidence that God's heaven will include within its confines the best exemplars of our cultural past, including dusty libraries and silent dirigibles, golden chariots and Chevy convertibles. And it leads me to suspect that a walk down to the shores of a heavenly Mediterranean will reveal the very best of Tarshish proudly moored to the dock, water lapping at its hull, waiting to sail once again. And if the ships of Tarshish, why not the

RMS *Titanic*? One day we may have the privilege of standing on the bow of that proud product of the shipyard of Dublin, restored for an eternity of service. But if we do have an opportunity to ride the resurrected *Titanic*, then (with apologies to Leonardo DiCaprio) we will surely use it as an opportunity to praise the *real* King of the world.

HEAVENLY QUESTIONS

1. Do you think the idea of cultural resurrection is plausible?
2. Are there any products of culture that you'd like to see resurrected to eternity? A favorite car? A painting? A house? A coffee shop?
3. If God does resurrect the *Titanic*, would you want to sail on it?

Question 12

Will God Resurrect Entire Cultural Neighborhoods?

If God will resurrect the best of human culture and technology, it won't be merely as a menagerie, an eclectic collection of bits thrown together on display. Rather, it will be in a meaningful, living whole. Does this mean that God will resurrect entire cultural environs? And what would that mean for the lowly video store?

If you ever have the chance to visit Banff, a charming resort town in the Canadian Rockies, I strongly suggest that you make time in your itinerary to drop in to the Banff Park Museum on the south end of Banff Avenue. The museum is unique because it faithfully maintains exhibits and displays that were current a century ago. In doing so, it effectively provides a time capsule *museum of a museum* that accurately conveys how the study of natural history was conceived in the early twentieth century.

As you may expect, it turns out that museums of a century ago were very different than they are today. The walls at the Banff Park Museum are crammed with a menagerie of stuffed animals. There doesn't seem to be any overarching rhyme or reason to the presentation. Voles, foxes, weasels, and raccoons crowd the walls. More animals are displayed in glass boxes with no discernible theme or logic—a giant beaver, a wolverine, a loon—while a large grizzly bear looms over the scene and an eagle peers down with glass eyes from a cedar rafter.

The design philosophy of Banff's historic museum is very different from museums and zoos today that pursue a much more holistic philosophy, seeking to embed displays within natural environments that invite the participation of visitors. In short, the goal of museums today is to create an immersion experience in order to draw the visitor into the past. This immersion design philosophy is reflected in Jon Coe and Greg Dykstra's exposition of the word *exhibit* in contemporary museum design. No longer is an exhibit an object or entity set in a glass case or mounted on a wall ready for clinical examination. Rather, they say:

> In the context of immersion design, the term has a broader meaning, including the entire environmental surround. This could include everything from the surfacing underfoot, to the themed character interacting with guests, to vistas of distant landscape.[1]

Needless to say, this contrasts markedly with the Banff Park Museum's reductionistic philosophy in which an exhibit is merely a collection of artifacts stuffed into glass boxes and mounted on walls. Today we recognize that the quest to understand the world is about much more than arbitrarily arranging a menagerie of items haphazardly in a display. Instead, we appreciate the importance of presenting living systems.

As we explore the vision of culture resurrected into eternity, we should be careful not to fall into the reductionistic errors of the Banff Park Museum. If we are to talk about the redemption of culture and technology, it will presumably involve more than God restoring a smattering of cultural artifacts—ships, houses, canoes, airships, chariots, books—plucked from the past and dropped into the glass display cases of a heavenly museum. Instead, a resurrected past will be holistic and immersive, allowing people to experience the best of redeemed culture. In the rest of this chapter I will explore this notion by focusing on a cultural institution that is currently in its final death throes due to the relentless march of technology: the video rental store.

The Video Rental Store? Seriously?

Even a few months ago it would never have occurred to me to *lament* the demise of the video store, still less to anticipate its eschatological reestablishment. Like many people, I stopped going to video stores a few years ago—about the same time that Blockbuster, the once mighty chain, began the steep decline from which it never recovered. In retrospect, the demise was inevitable, as any moderately skilled futurist could have predicted. In a universe of Netflix, Redbox, iTunes, Pirate Bay, and pay-per-view television, the days of the once ubiquitous cultural institution known as the neighborhood video store were numbered.

So it was something of a novelty one evening in January 2012 when my friend suggested that we visit his neighborhood video store, a modest joint called Videodrome. *Video* store? I hadn't been in a video store for a couple years. In fact, I had sort of assumed by now they'd gone the way of the dodo. "Sure," I replied, my curiosity piqued. "Let's see what they've got."

The first thing that hit me after walking in the door was that distinctive video store aroma that I'd all but forgotten—a heady, stale mixture of cheap plastic, Berber carpet, and popcorn. A black-and-white film from Hollywood's golden era was playing on the television monitor. As I began to walk the aisles, I realized how *right* it felt to browse titles on a shelf, surrounded by the smell of cheap plastic and popcorn and the sound of a movie playing in the background. Suddenly I was reliving the Saturday evening ritual of a bygone era.

Bygone indeed. The gentleman sitting behind the counter appeared amiable, knowledgeable, quirky . . . and slightly bored. Yes, bored. Glancing around the store I could get a sense for why: though it was a Saturday night, there were only about a half dozen people milling about the aisles pensively scanning the racks of DVDs and VHS videotapes. (Yes, they actually still had VHS tapes! But alas, no Beta.)

As I stood there, the sensory overload invoked in me a deep sense of nostalgia. While video stores may be all but extinct, they have played an important role in the cultural Zeitgeist of the modern West. In his memoirs, Nathan Rabin reflects on working at a Blockbuster video store as a teenager. He recalls that on his first day of employment he viewed a training video that welcomed him to the "entertainment industry." While he never bought into the propaganda that a minimum-wage video clerk was really part of the entertainment industrial complex, he still looked back warmly at his time working at the store. As he recalls, "Talking about movies freed me from my crippling self-consciousness. Movies were liberating. They made me feel alive and pointed to a wonderful world." Looking back, he reminisces on the promise of that time in his life:

> Working at Blockbuster gave me an opportunity to be around my beloved movies. It was a tawdry, for-profit cathedral of film. Every video box radiated promise. As a kid, I used to go to video stores and fantasize dreamily about all the films I'd see someday. Now I had unfettered access to a treasure trove of classics.[2]

With the video store now in its final death throes, Rabin worries about the next generation: "I fear that Netflix will breed a generation of cinephiles and filmmakers who will be more obsessive and informed than their predecessors but also even more removed from human contact."[3] Rabin has reason to worry. Netflix may be more efficient than the video store, but that efficiency is gained at the loss of significant interaction with one's wider community.

As I stood there in the entrance to Videodrome, I was suddenly flooded with memories from the countless video stores I'd visited over my life. I remembered back in 1984 standing in the aisles of Silver Screen Video with our babysitter, trying to convince her that John Carpenter's *Halloween* was actually a documentary about the autumn holiday rather than a classic slasher flick. (It didn't work.) By the time I hit high school I usually rented from the local convenience store where I regularly hung out with friends. It was there that I became familiar with an eclectic mix of artistically substandard movies like Clint Eastwood's *Pink Cadillac* and the black comedy *Weekend at Bernie's*.

A decade later I was living in London with my wife while completing my doctorate in theology. Given that it was tough to find budget entertainment in that famously expensive city, we were delighted to discover a little video store near our house with a treasure trove of international films available to rent at *two* movies for a pound. It was there that we discovered countless great works of the British, Iranian, and French cinema.

Over the last decade of the video store, I settled down into a comfortable suburban life back in North America, and that inevitably meant Blockbuster. With a young daughter now in tow, my wife and I were introduced to a range of first-rate children's films from the likes of Pixar and Studio Ghibli (a Japanese animation house). And while standing in those interminably long Friday night checkout lines, we were coerced into buying countless confections—licorice, chocolate, popcorn. But we didn't mind; it was all part of the experience.

Now as all those memories flooded back at the entrance to Videodrome, I felt a sadness in realizing that the demise of the video store had brought an entire part of my life to an end . . . and I hadn't even noticed.

Netflix and Redbox and pay-per-view had certainly made life easier. They were technologically streamlined, efficient, and for the most part, more economical. But Rabin was right: these efficiencies were achieved at the high cost of eliminating human contact and leaving people sitting on their couches. For the first time I began to appreciate what had been lost with the demise of the video store. As one video store owner recalled of the golden days of video: "You [could] spend a length of a movie trying to find something with your friends. It was like a little event."[4] Alas, there's nothing eventful about scrolling through the menu on Netflix.

A Hope that the Video Store Lives Again

Before I am accused of a woolly sentimentalism, let me acknowledge that we need to be careful about uncritically romanticizing the past, and that includes the video store. Joshua Greenberg reminds us of the frustrations that came with video stores—paramount of which was failing to find the film you were looking for.[5] And don't forget the endlessly accumulating late fees for a movie forgotten behind the couch. ("I was *sure* I returned that!") Nor does Rabin remember with fondness the minimum wage Blockbuster paid. Unlike the *real* entertainment industry, nobody working at a video store got rich.[6]

The point is not that the video store was perfect or that it should be idealized. Rather, the point is that despite its imperfections, it brought much communal good—good that has been lost with the ever-advancing march of technology. Consequently, it is a reasonable hope that someday the video store, and the goodness that it brought, may be resurrected to perfection.

Could the video store live again? If it will, it will likely be not as an artifact in a glass case but rather as part of an immersive design philosophy. What does this mean exactly? Well to start with, it means that the restored Videodrome will not be a museum piece dropped into an eclectic cultural menagerie between an eighteenth-century English teahouse and a sixteenth-century Salish longhouse. If it lives again, it will be as a *functioning* video store serving *a community*.

If we are to think of a restored community video store, it requires that we think of a holistic and immersive cultural neighborhood into which it is embedded. To get a handle on this idea, we should think for a moment of Disneyland. This classic theme park is composed of several sections, each with a unified theme and set in a particular temporal period such as Frontierland, Tomorrowland, and Main Street, U.S.A. Each represents an immersive environment that draws the visitor in for a complete experience. If Walt Disney can do it, surely God can pull off something infinitely greater.

So it may very well be that the resurrection of creation will likewise involve countless immersive *exhibits*—complex, interrelated cultural environments representing the best of human cultural history. If the English teahouse lives again, we can reasonably expect it to do so not as a model assembled within a glass case and left to collect dust, but as an establishment within an appropriate cultural environ, replete with the cobblestones and period dress of eighteenth-century England. And the Salish longhouse reborn will not be restored to sit in a dusty museum but rather will be nestled in the midst of towering, Pacific-coast cedars on a misty, gray shoreline.

And what about the video store? Perhaps heaven will see a Videodrome (or a Silver Screen or a Blockbuster) restored to a period neighborhood embodying the culture and technology of 1990s North America—along with a bustling arcade and a real, bona fide phone booth on the corner.

And what would this mean for the communal restoration of the venerable video store that once succeeded in making the rental of a film into a communal event? While it is difficult to imagine what this may mean, we can guess that as a restored video store would bring the best from the past, so it would have its many imperfections eliminated. And you know what that means: *no more late fees*.

Heavenly Questions

1. Do you have fond memories of video stores? If there are video stores in heaven, will you visit one? And how do you think it will be different?

2. What other cultural institutions of a bygone era would you like to see again?

3. Do you think this idea of an immersion into a redeemed cultural history makes sense? If God does redeem entire cultural neighborhoods, then in which time and place would you choose to reside most often and why?

Question 13

Will God Resurrect Insects?

Most people take the query of whether all dogs will go to heaven with a surprising degree of seriousness. Well, perhaps it isn't that surprising: When people love their companion animals—dogs, cats, birds, horses—it is natural for them to hope to see those beloved companions again. But what about creatures less likely to be the objects of human affection, like cockroaches, mosquitoes, and spiders? Will God raise up insects to populate heaven?

When James Dobson was thirteen, his father unexpectedly pulled him out of school in the middle of the day. It was a moment that Jim will never forget. The instant that he saw his father's pained expression, he knew that something was terribly wrong. Immediately gripped with fear, he asked whether his mom was okay. When his father nodded, Jim then turned his concern to his beloved dog. What about Pippy?

Then came the dreaded news. Mr. Dobson gently explained that the loving little dog had been accidentally run over by Jim's mother. After she felt the sickening bump, she ran out of the car and found Pippy lying in the street, his little back broken. Despite his critical state, he managed to wag his stubby little tail when he saw her. Moments later he was gone.

Dobson reflects on the fierce pain that gripped him with this great loss:

> Now it may not seem too terrible to lose a dog, but Pippy's death was like the end of the world for me. I simply cannot describe how important he was to me when I was thirteen years old. He was my very special friend whom I loved more than anyone can imagine. I could talk to him about things that no one else seemed to understand. He met me on the edge of the sidewalk after school each day and wagged his tail to greet me (which no one else ever did for me). I would take him out in the backyard and we would play and run together. He was always in a good mood, even when I was not. Yes, Pippy and I had something going between us that only dog lovers can comprehend.[1]

Looking back all these years later, Dobson still struggles to put into words all that Pippy meant to him and how deeply he was impacted by the loss: "When my father told me this story of Pippy's death, I thought I was going to die. I couldn't swallow and I found it very hard to breathe. I wanted to run away . . . to scream . . . to cry."[2]

The Love of a Pet

I know what that kind of loss is like. When I was ten years old, my dad picked me up from school with a somber look on his face. My beloved cockatiel, Pippins, had been sick, and my father's expression told me everything I needed to know. Immediately I slid onto the floor of the car, bawling.

Pippins was an amazing little bird. He loved being close to people. With every pat on his little head he chirped softly and sidled up closer to the present object of his affection until he was beak to nose. Every time we arrived home, he let the whole neighborhood know by shrieking joyously in his cage. He enjoyed placidly perching on the lampshade (and pooping down the inside of it) as he magisterially surveyed the entire living room. Most of all he loved nibbling the edge of my leather Bible when I wasn't looking. So many precious memories . . . and now he was gone.

Other people have profound relationships with various other kinds of companion animals. One young girl named Gabrielle speaks simply but profoundly of her love for her cat Zeus: "He's my favorite cat. He's a gift from God."[3] And George MacDonald, the great fantasy writer of the nineteenth century, had a particularly deep connection to his horses. In the following passage he reflects on the love of animals:

> Your dog, your horse tells you about him who cares for all his creatures. None of them came from his hands. Perhaps the precious things of the earth, the coal and the diamonds, the iron and clay and gold, may be said to have come from his hands; but the live things come from his heart—from near the same region whence ourselves we came. How much my horse may, in his own fashion—that is, God's equine way—know of him, I cannot tell, because he cannot tell. Also, we do not know what the horses know, because they are horses, and we are at best, in relation to them, only horsemen. The ways of God go down into microscopic depths, as well as up into telescopic heights—and with more marvel, for there lie the beginnings of life: the immensities of stars and worlds all exist for the sake of less things than they. So with mind; the ways of God go into the depths yet unrevealed to us; he knows his horses and dogs as we cannot know them, because we are not yet pure sons of God.[4]

Christians have often been very careful about speculating on the lives of God's creatures for fear of being charged with anthropomorphism and sentimentalism. "Your horse doesn't really love you." "That dog isn't really mourning the loss of its owner." "Your cat doesn't even know you exist." "You're just projecting human emotions onto the beasts." On the contrary, MacDonald suggests that the real problem is not that we project too much but rather that we perceive too little. Other creatures are known and loved by God—the one who created them and sustains them. It is only because we have not yet reached our glorified status as true sons and daughters of God that we fail to perceive this truth.

Do All Dogs Go to Heaven? Do Any?

What are the prospects of other creatures being restored again to enjoy an even more profound relationship with us? Could Pippy be there to play with James Dobson again? And what about my cockatiel, Pippins? Will he again nibble the edges of my Bible? Will Gabrielle's cat again climb the scratching post? And will George MacDonald's beloved horses once again trot through open pastureland?

While there is definitely some plausibility to the notion of many companion animals being resurrected, most people today probably assume that dogs are the best candidates for resurrection. As the saying goes, *all dogs go to heaven*. And they are "man's best friend," aren't they? So you may be surprised to know that the typical ancient Israelite would not have put dogs anywhere near the top of the list of animals likely to be resurrected. You see, the Israelites didn't view dogs as cherished family companions. Rather, they usually viewed dogs as dirty scavengers.[5] As a result, references to dogs in the Bible tend to be quite negative (e.g., 2 Sam. 3:8; 1 Kings 21:19; 2 Kings 8:13; Ps. 22:20; Prov. 26:11). Given that nothing impure will enter the kingdom of God (Rev. 21:27), and dogs are explicitly mentioned as outside the New Jerusalem (Rev. 22:15), it is doubtful that most Israelites would have envisioned seeing these dirty canine scavengers in heaven.

What do we learn from the Israelites' view of dogs? The biblical writers may have generally held negative attitudes toward dogs, but that's very different from saying the Bible *teaches* a negative attitude toward dogs. The fact is that people today are aware of the value of dogs in a way that most Israelites simply were not. As a result, we are more sensitive to the role they could play in God's salvation plan for creation.

There is a lesson here for us. If the Israelites failed to appreciate the place of dogs in God's creation plan, it is likely that *we* often fail to appreciate the place of other creatures. It is now time to consider one notable example.

Insects in Heaven?

First, let's be clear on one thing: it is inexcusably anthropocentric to assume that God is only interested in the destiny of animals with which humans have bothered to develop personal relationships. So while reflections on companion animals may provide a good launching point for consideration of the future of other creatures, our vision for creation will be impoverished if we limit our vision to resurrected pets. If God will restore other creatures, it will not be simply because we loved them but because *he* loves them. Nor should it be any surprise that God loves his creatures. If he loved us while we were yet sinners (Rom. 5:8), surely he can love a dog while it is yet a scavenger.

While there are many candidates we may like to exclude from heaven (rodents and snakes for starters), perhaps the best candidate of all are insects (and other creatures we consider bugs). Granted, most people are willing to make a few six-legged exceptions. For example, we may welcome ladybugs, butterflies, and crickets into the kingdom. (Ralph Waldo Emerson once likened the chirp of the snowy tree cricket to the silent dance of the moonlight rendered audible.[6]) But for most of us, the goodwill disappears with the thought of mosquitoes, cockroaches, and spiders buzzing and crawling into the dark and dusty corners of the new creation. Is this feeling justified, or should we expect to see the full gamut of bugs as surely as we will see the entire spectrum of dog breeds?

C. S. Lewis famously addressed the eschatological home of mosquitoes by observing, "If the worst came to the worst, a heaven for mosquitoes and a hell for men could very conveniently be combined."[7] While this is an eminently quotable passage, it unfortunately forgoes a direct answer for the sake of a clever turn of phrase. So we will forgo the temptation to settle the matter by quoting Lewis and move on by pressing for a clearer and more adequate response.

We can begin to address this by asking whether insects are important to creation. One way to gauge the place of insects in creation is by considering how many insect species there are in the world. The idea is that the more insects we find now, the more we will likely see them in the new creation. By that reasoning, I have some bad news: this world has *a lot* of bugs. Just consider beetles for starters. When scientist John Haldane was asked what we could infer about God from study of the natural world, he famously quipped, "An inordinate fondness for beetles."[8] The statistics back Haldane up. According to the best estimates, the earth has at least *350,000 species of beetles.*[9]

Nor are God's interests limited to beetles. Insects generally seem to have caught his creative imagination. While there are approximately one million named insect species, estimates are that there are an additional five to ten million species still unknown to science. Incredibly, insects make up approximately 90 percent of the distinct species on earth.[10] If we shift from counting species to weighing biomass, insects still come out as important since the biomass of all the insects on earth outweighs the human species *sixfold.*[11]

The importance is amplified further if we consider the central role of insects in the ecosystems in which they live. For example, consider that the economic impact of the colony collapse disorder that ravaged American beehives in 2006–2007 cost the US agricultural economy between $8 and $12 billion.[12] And that's just *bees.* As those staggering numbers indicate, calling insects important to the ecosystems in which they live is an understatement.

To put it simply, if God loved insects enough to fill his planet with them the first time around, we have excellent reasons to expect he'll do so again. From that perspective, the news is even worse for the insectophobe, because we have no reason to assume that God will limit himself to restoring the insects currently living on the earth. If he resurrects presently existing insects, he may very well resurrect long-extinct insects as well, like the mighty *Meganeura*, a prehistoric dragonfly the size of a bird, and *Arthropleura*, a prehistoric centipede that measured *eight feet long*. Who knows what other six-, eight-, or one hundred–legged wonders may be waiting to greet us in the darkened corners of eternity!

Learning to Love Insects

With all this to look forward to, we may as well begin developing our respect and admiration for insects now. And a good place to start is by spending some time with the great eighteenth-century theologian Jonathan Edwards. It has been said that Edwards was God-intoxicated, for he could find the divine majesty in the most unexpected places. One of those surprising places is displayed in his famous "Spider Letter" of October 31, 1723, which describes "the wondrous and curious works of the spider."[13]

Edwards begins by discoursing eloquently on the beauty of spider webs. But it is not just the webs that fascinate him. He is equally taken by the way the spiders seem to *enjoy* their work: "That which is most astonishing is that very often there appears at the end of these webs, spiders sailing in the air with them, doubtless with abundance of pleasure."[14]

Edwards may well be guilty of some anthropomorphic projection here, but there are worse crimes. And we can definitely learn something from his unrestrained pleasure in the "amazing works" of the lowly arachnid. This is a Psalm 19 moment as Edwards moves from marveling at the works of the spider to praising "the exuberant goodness of the Creator, who hath not only provided for all the necessities, but also for the pleasure and recreation of all sorts of creatures, even the insects."[15]

The lesson is that we don't get to pick and choose which aspects of creation we will see again in eternity. Since God loved it all and declared it all good, our view of the new creation should always err on the side of superabundance. As a result, we have good reason to believe that just as the ancient Israelite will come to welcome Dobson's dog Pippy into the new creation, so will it be that the arachnids we once sought to crush with a broom, we will one day welcome with all the enthusiasm of Jonathan Edwards.

Heavenly Questions

1. Have you ever loved a companion animal? If so, how do you feel about the prospect of seeing that companion in heaven?

2. Why do you think God created so many different kinds of insects? Do you think God has a particular fondness for insects?

3. Are there any creatures that you would rather not see in heaven? Snakes? Rats? Cockroaches? Bedbugs? Do you think it is possible to find God's handiwork even in those creatures?

Question 14

Will Tigers Still Hunt Wild Boar?

The great predators are surely among the grandest and most impressive creatures in creation. But their role in the new creation will be radically transformed to a peaceable existence with those creatures that were once their prey. And this raises a difficult question: Is a tiger that has gone vegan still a tiger?

The story opens with twelve-year-old Rob Horton out wandering in the woods near his home at the Kentucky Star Motel, just off the highway in Florida. Suddenly he comes on a great iron cage deep in the forest. That in itself is surprising enough. But even more remarkable is what Rob finds lurking within: "Inside the cage, unbelievably, there was a tiger—a real-life, very large tiger pacing back and forth. He was orange and gold and so bright, it was like staring at the sun itself, angry and trapped in a cage."[1] So begins Kate DiCamillo's children's novel *The Tiger Rising*.

As the story unfolds, Rob and his friend Sistine cannot stand the thought of seeing the tiger kept in the cage, so they begin to formulate a plan to liberate it. Willie May, the kind old lady who works at the hotel, warns them not to proceed with their plan. She tells them that Florida is no place for a tiger. Even the panthers once native to the region have long since disappeared.[2] And if there is no room for a panther, there *certainly* isn't room for a tiger.

But the children don't heed Willie May's reasoned entreaties. Throwing caution to the wind, one day Rob steals the keys for the cage from Beauchamp, the tiger's owner, and he goes with Sistine to free the creature. After unlocking the cage, they bravely swing open the iron gate and wait.

> As they stared, the tiger stepped with grace and delicacy out of the cage. He put his nose up and sniffed. He took one tiny step and then another. Then he stopped and stood still. Sistine clapped her hands, and the tiger turned and looked back at them both, his eyes blazing. And then he started to run.
>
> He ran so fast, it looked to Rob like he was flying. His muscles moved like a river; it was hard to believe that a cage had ever contained him.[3]

It is a wonderful moment as a tiger is allowed to be a tiger again.

But the euphoric experience of liberation does not last long. Moments later Rob and Sistine hear screams and then the crack of a gun. The children run in the direction of the shouting and, horrified, they find Rob's father standing grimly with his shotgun. There at his feet lies the tiger, dead.

It is at that moment that we realize the ironic tragedy of the situation: In their well-intentioned attempt to liberate the great cat, Rob and Sistine instead sealed its destruction. Willie May was right, but Rob and Sistine didn't listen. They could only see the need to liberate the tiger from the cage. They couldn't see that doing so would bring its death.

But Won't the Tigers Be Saved?

Perhaps you're wondering why I'm bothering to share Rob and Sistine's misbegotten efforts to free the tiger. The reason is because their story conveys something of the dilemma Christians face when thinking about the redemption of the great predators. The danger is that in much the same way that Rob and Sistine's efforts to free the tiger from its cage resulted in its destruction, so our concerns for eternal redemption for the great predators threatens to result in their destruction.

I admit that this claim is a surprising one. After all, Scripture describes the great predators as being *redeemed*: "The wolf will live with the lamb, the leopard will lie down with the goat, the calf and the lion and the yearling together; and a little child will lead them" (Isa. 11:6). Moreover, we are assured, "The wolf and the lamb will feed together, and the lion will eat straw like the ox" (Isa. 65:25). These are images of peace and salvation, not destruction and death. Christopher Wright comments:

> No longer will there be . . . polarization in the new creation. There will be peaceful coexistence among animals as well as between animals and humans. For there will be no more harm or destruction in the new creation. No more death is the promise for animals as much as for humans. Death in all its forms will be nonexistent, not even a memory in the new creation.[4]

Far from being destroyed, wolves, leopards, lions, and tigers will flourish in the new creation, and apparently they'll do so as peaceable herbivores. So what's the problem?

The Parable of the Tiger That Became a Fish

The problem is precisely with the promise that great predators will become peaceable herbivores. We can illustrate it with a parable:

> There once was a valley that was being inundated by the rising waters of the sea. As the waters began to fill every piece of land, the animals scurried up to higher ground. One after the other the monkeys, lemurs, and boars all made their way up the steep slopes of the valley to live life on the cliffs above.
>
> Alas, the proud tiger was too clumsy to scale the steep walls and too large to live on the narrow cliffs above the valley. And so he remained in the middle of the jungle helplessly calling out for aid as the waters rolled in all around him.
>
> The Forest Fairy heard the cries of the mighty tiger and came down to the valley. "I have heard your cries, Mr. Tiger. And I will save you from the rising waters," the Forest Fairy said. "I see that you are too clumsy to climb the walls of the valley and too large to live on the cliffs above. So I will save you from the rising waters by turning you into a fish instead."
>
> And so it was. That very moment the tiger was turned into a tuna and dropped into the rising waters. And he lived out his days swimming in the flooded valley.

Is that a happy ending? That depends on whether you think the tiger was actually saved when the Forest Fairy turned it into a fish. I admit that I'm skeptical about that. Perhaps another illustration can explain my skepticism more clearly. Imagine that your neighbor is a well-intentioned but inept magician who one day inadvertently floods your backyard while doing renovations on his Olympic-sized swimming pool. You are horrified when you return home and find your backyard submerged in three feet of water. "My teacup poodle was in the backyard!" you wail. "Don't worry," the magician replies with a grin. "I saved your dog from the flood of water—by turning it into a guppy." And with that he hands you a fish in a bucket of water. Would you think the magician had saved your dog by changing it into a fish? Presumably the answer is: *only if he changes it back again.*

Big Cats Turned into Cows?

The magician illustration strongly suggests that you can't save a dog or tiger by irreversibly turning it into a fish any more than you can save a man by turning him into a tree. But how is that relevant to the Bible? After all, Isaiah's prophecies don't describe God as transforming great predators into *fish* (unless, as in the case with sharks, they were fish to begin with). Rather, the texts suggest that he leaves them a lot like they were before—*sans* their predatory nature. The lion will remain a lion except for its new vegetarian diet.

A closer look, however, suggests that the change will be more radical than you may initially suppose. To begin with, the radical shift in the lion's diet would alter its appearance. Its dentition and jaw would have to be significantly changed to allow it to eat grass instead of meat, to say nothing of the radical reworking of its internal organs. Even more striking, if harder to quantify, would be the radical alteration in (or eradication of?) the leonine nature. George Adamson writes, "A lion is not a lion if it is only free to eat, to sleep and to copulate. It deserves to be free to hunt and to choose its own prey; to look for and find its own mate; to fight for and hold its own territory; and to die where it was born—in the wild."[5] In Adamson's estimation, being a great cat means maintaining the fearsome predatory nature of a great cat. Consequently, if you turn a great cat into a benign herbivore, the cat, for all intents and purposes, has been replaced by something altogether different.

There certainly is something majestic about the great predators. Consider the famous scene in *The Lion, the Witch and the Wardrobe* where Susan asks the Beavers if Aslan the lion is safe. "'Safe?' said Mr. Beaver; 'don't you hear what Mrs. Beaver tells you? Who said anything about safe? 'Course he isn't safe. But he's good.'"[6] There is an excellent reason that Lewis describes Aslan as the kind of lion we're familiar with rather than a cow (or for that matter, a domesticated lion). A fierce, predatory lion has presence; it has *gravitas*. A cud-chewing lion just isn't the same.

The same applies to the other great predators. The point then is not that the tiger released into the new creation is transformed into something as radically different as a fish. But its redemption as a cow-like, hybrid creature would be extraordinarily radical nonetheless. And when you turn a tiger into a ruminant hybrid that lies in a field lazily chewing its cud, haven't you essentially replaced the great cat with something altogether different? Being a tiger is about being a hunter—a ferocious, unpredictable predator with presence, as DiCamillo's children's book eloquently describes. Is there a way to release the tiger from the cage of a groaning creation without losing that which makes the tiger so majestic?[7]

Whether we're talking about tigers or lions, leopard seals or wolves, cheetahs or polar bears, eagles or killer whales, in each case something of the glory and beauty of these creatures is found in their identity as mighty predators. As a result, it seems something essential will be lost if we declare that once-proud predators will one day be content munching grass lazily beside a pack of plump, snoring, meaty morsels.

Heavenly Hunting for Sport?

Is there a way to maintain something of the glory of the one-time predator inside the peaceable kingdom? To what extent could a tiger or lion retain its predatory nature?

Here's a possibility. Perhaps the tiger's predatory nature toward certain prey will not be eradicated but rather channeled into a form of benign sport akin to animals playing capture the flag or paintball. As a result, the tortured, predatory, life-and-death struggle we now see will be wiped away, but the best part of a tiger's predatory majesty will remain. It may even look like this:

As the people watch quietly from the Land Rover, the wild boar walks up to the oasis and eyes the surrounding landscape. It all looks clear. But the people know it is not. The tiger has been lying in wait for a while now, hidden in the tall grass. The boar cautiously makes its way down to the water and begins to drink. As the breeze picks up, there is movement in the grass and a gasp goes through the audience. At that moment a flash of orange emerges in a flurry of movement. The great predator leaps from the bushes as the boar turns to bolt. But it is too late. The tiger cuffs the boar's flank. Down goes the boar as the tiger leaps on him, triumphantly placing his mouth on the creature's neck in a menacing pose. Applause erupts from the Land Rover as the great cat steps back triumphantly, allowing the boar to hop up and run off for another competition on another day.

Score one for the tiger.

HEAVENLY QUESTIONS

1. Do you think that predators have their own magnificence in virtue of being predators?

2. Do you think animals like tigers became predators because of the sin of Adam? If so, how do you think that happened?

3. What do you think of the idea that predators could retain their predatory nature as a form of sport? Is that a plausible idea or a silly one? (Don't worry, you can call it silly if you like. I can take it.)

Part 4

Relationships Perfected

According to the heavenly equation, the relationships that God's creatures have with one another and with God himself will be perfected as well. But what will these perfected relationships look like? We will explore that question by seeking to understand how we will relate to God, to other people, to other intelligent life forms, and to our very selves.

Question 15

Will We Walk with Jesus in the Garden?

At the heart of the promise and hope of heaven is the prospect of sharing intimate communion with Jesus. But what will it mean to have communion with the incarnate Jesus? Christians have not reflected often enough on the way that the incarnation places practical constraints on how we will relate to Christ in eternity.

And He walks with me, and He talks with me,
And He tells me I am His own;
And the joy we share as we tarry there,
None other has ever known.[1]

So goes the chorus of one of the most beloved of modern hymns, "In the Garden," by Charles Austin Miles. We may not all find a walk in a garden equally appealing—personally I'd prefer to have a coffee with Jesus at a sidewalk café—but all Christians share the desire for intimate communion with their Lord. Max Lucado writes, "Heaven invites you to set the lens of your heart on the heart of the Savior and make him the object of your life."[2] The question before us is concerned with the form that this communion will take in light of the fact that Christ is eternally incarnate. Christians often fail to appreciate the significance of this question because they've not grasped the full, radical implications of the incarnation.

Finding Jesus in *The Shack*

The storied success of William Paul Young's bestselling novel, *The Shack*, is well-known.[3] Independently published on a shoestring budget, the book went on to sell well in excess of ten million copies. The novel tells the fictional story of Mack, a man who is struggling to come to terms with the horrific murder of his daughter Missy at the hands of a serial killer. One day Mack receives a letter in the mail that appears to be an invitation to visit the very shack where Missy was murdered. The letter is signed "Papa," the name by which Mack's wife refers to God the Father. Against his better judgment, Mack travels alone to the cabin in the woods and apprehensively walks up to the door of the cabin. Just as he is about to turn around and leave, the door swings open and he is embraced by a large African American woman who calls herself Papa. Meet God the Father. Soon after, Mack meets an Asian woman named Sarayu, who, it turns out, is the Holy Spirit.

As a result of the provocative portrayal, Young was charged by some critics with idolatry. The charge is an ironic one given that the point of depicting God in female form was precisely to *challenge* the tendency toward idolatry. You see, by depicting God as Papa and Sarayu, Young is reminding us that all our experience of God is an accommodation in which God comes into our framework of understanding to make himself comprehensible in terms we can grasp.[4] This is necessary given that God utterly transcends our understanding (Isa. 55:8–9).

The necessity of accommodation is memorably illustrated by Philip Yancey when he describes the time he kept an aquarium. Despite all his work laboring faithfully to ensure that his fish flourished in the tank, whenever he drew close to the aquarium, the fish swam quickly away. Yancey reflects:

> To my fish I was deity. I was too large for them, my actions too incomprehensible. My acts of mercy they saw as cruelty; my attempts at healing they viewed as destruction. To change their perceptions, I began to see, would require a form of incarnation. I would have to become a fish and "speak" to them in a language they could understand.[5]

This is a great summary of accommodation in which one individual seeks to enter into the limited experience of another to make understanding possible.

This is precisely what God does for each of us: he accommodates his truth in terms that we can understand and meets us where we are. God came to the Israelites through a pillar of cloud by day and a pillar of fire by night. He came to Elijah through the mighty wind and the still small voice. He comes to defeated people everywhere as a protector and father.

God's pattern of accommodation is provocatively illustrated in *The Shack*. While Mack is definitely defeated, he is unable to relate to God as Father because of abuse he suffered at the hand of his human father. And so God accommodates just for him as an African American woman named Papa and an Asian woman named Sarayu.

Since Young is so provocative in portraying the Father and Spirit, it may be something of a surprise that this creative play disappears when it comes to his depiction of Jesus. Far from adopting an equally novel and surprising form, Jesus appears to Mack precisely as you'd expect—a Jewish man of average looks. Why the conventional portrayal? Did Young just run out of ideas when he got to the Second Person of the Trinity?

Far from it. Instead, the point is that the first-century, Jewish male form of accommodation assumed by God the Son is not merely another ad hoc accommodation that God assumes temporarily for a particular time and place. Rather, it is an actual incarnation, a case of God the Son *becoming* a man named Jesus. Mack recognizes that Jesus is different during his weekend in the cabin, for Jesus appears to be "more real or tangible" than either Papa or Sarayu. And Jesus points out to Mack, "Since I am human we have much in common to begin with."[6] The different nature of Jesus's accommodation is vividly captured in Mack's observation that while a hug from Papa or Sarayu has an ethereal quality about it, a hug from Jesus *feels* like a hug.[7]

Unfortunately, Christians often fail to grasp the radical extent of accommodation proposed by the doctrine of incarnation. So let's be clear: The claim is not simply that just as God the Father became a pillar of fire every evening for the Israelites, so God the Son became the human Jesus for a few decades and then sloughed off humanity when he ascended back to the Father's right hand. Rather, Scripture teaches that God the Son *really became* the man Jesus (John 1:14), and he never left this human nature behind. Jesus is raised with a physical, human resurrection body and ascends to his Father's right hand as that human being (Luke 24:51). After the ascension, Scripture continues to describe Jesus as a man (1 Tim. 2:5) who will return as the Son of Man (Matt. 16:27; Acts 1:11).[8] Clearly Jesus is not simply another accommodation. Rather, the incarnation is the apogee of accommodation, the point at which God, in God the Son, actually *becomes* the form of accommodation rather than merely adopting it for a time.

Jesus in Eternity

Since Jesus is our once-for-all mediator (1 Tim. 2:5; Heb. 7:11–28), it is through him that we can approach the Father's throne (Eph. 3:12). It is no surprise, then, that in practical terms our relationship with Jesus will be central to our experience of the Triune God eternally. But how will we relate to Jesus given that he is both fully divine and fully human? We will begin by considering what it will mean to relate to Jesus as divine before we turn to the central question of relating to him as an incarnate man.

To affirm that Jesus is divine is to affirm that he is omnipresent. But what does it actually mean to be omnipresent? People often assume that being omnipresent means you are *physically* everywhere. That is a mistake, albeit an understandable one. Properly understood, omnipresence doesn't include any notion of *physical* presence. Rather, an agent is omnipresent in virtue of being omniscient (having all knowledge) and omnipotent (having all power). Since God is both omniscient (he knows everything that occurs) and omnipotent (he has power over everything that occurs), we say that he is therefore omnipresent.

Theologians have long debated the question of whether, or in what way, God the Son was omniscient and omnipotent during his life and ministry recorded in the Gospels. But we can all agree that he is definitely omniscient and omnipotent now and will be for eternity. Consequently, when we are glorified in eternity, we will enjoy an un-filtered experience of Christ's divine omnipresence. This will mean, for example, that a prayer in eternity will be met with an immediacy and intimacy that we cannot presently fathom.

While it is an exciting prospect to envision this kind of unfiltered, intimate relationship with Jesus, the sentiment expressed in the hymn "In the Garden" is not simply the hope that we will relate to Jesus as the omnipresent, divine Son of God who knows our thoughts and has power over our actions. The sentiment is also the hope that we will relate to him intimately as the incarnate Son of Man who is physically present to do things with us, such as walking in a garden or drinking coffee in a bistro.

It is here that we immediately run into the practical limitations of being human. As omnipresent deity, Jesus is everywhere in virtue of having all knowledge and power, but *as incarnate man he can only be in one place at one time.* This places a strict limitation on the way Jesus can be present to people, for if Jesus is right now with you over there, then he cannot also be with me right here. Of course Jesus could appear in a christophany simultaneously at multiple places, perhaps like a holographic image. He could even create material replicas of his body and operate them remotely as if he were in each place. But in terms of real, incarnate presence—the body that once walked the dusty streets of Jerusalem and died for our sins—he can only be in one place at a time. (And just in case you're wondering, his apparent ability to pass through solid doors, seen in John 20:26, doesn't mean that he can be in two places at once.)

Practically speaking, this means that people will have to *take turns* enjoying intimate communion with Jesus. Consequently, while I can pray to him anytime, if he is presently walking with you in the garden, he cannot simultaneously be having an espresso with me at the bistro.

Planning a Day with Jesus

Let's take a moment to put these practical constraints into some perspective. In heaven there will be a lot of people wanting to spend time with Jesus. How many? That depends on how many people there are in heaven. For the sake of illustration, let's assume that there are exactly ten billion people in heaven. In addition, let's assume that we have all agreed to take turns having one twenty-four-hour earth day with Jesus. (No doubt we will often spend time with Jesus in groups as well. I'm offering this simplified scenario merely for illustrative purposes.) Based on those two assumptions, it would follow that after a day spent with Jesus, each denizen of heaven would have to wait in line another ten billion days, or *27,397,260 years*, before his or her next special day with Jesus would come around. That's one way to put the implications of Christ's humanity into proper perspective.

Granted, twenty-seven million years is a long time to wait for a walk in the garden (or an espresso at a bistro). But don't be discouraged. We can close this discussion off by considering two important points of good news.

To begin with, don't forget that we will be in heaven, so however long it may be between our times of intimate communion with incarnate Jesus, there will always be untold wonders to experience in the interim. Suffice it to say that nobody will be left sitting in a waiting room reading out-of-date copies of *People* magazine.

Further, we should also keep in mind that one of the great things about eternity is that it is an infinite period of time. This means that even if we have to wait twenty-seven million years for each day that we get to visit with incarnate Jesus, eternity will include not only an infinite number of twenty-seven million–year periods, but also an infinite number of days with Jesus for each of us. In other words, in eternity *each of us will have an infinite number of special days to spend with Jesus*, walking in the garden, sipping espresso at a bistro, and simply communing with the incarnate Creator and Savior of the world.

Heavenly Questions

1. What do you think about the idea that God the Son's incarnation is eternal?

2. Do you think we'll pray to God in heaven? What do you think it will be like to relate to Jesus?

3. What would you most like to do with Jesus on a special day?

Question 16

Will We Love Everyone the Same, or Will We Have Special Friends?

Few things in life can match the value of a good friend. There is something truly wonderful in having special people in your life who share your interests, your experiences, and of course your sense of humor. Given that special friends are so wonderful, will we have special friends in heaven? Or will everybody be our special friend?

As I said in the last chapter, in heaven we can look forward to spending an infinite number of days with Jesus. So it is a good thing that he calls us his friends (John 15:15). This incredible confession reminds us that at the core of the Christian hope is *friendship*, given the peace with God we have through Jesus (Rom. 5:1). While our eternal friendships are founded on a restored relationship with God, through that incredible reality we gain friendship with all other human beings as well. And that brings us to our next question.

When it comes to discussing our eternal friendships, one thing is beyond dispute: in heaven our relationships will be restored and perfected as the sinfulness that presently hampers our relations with one another is at last removed. Consequently, we will know friendship

121

as we have never known it before, free of gossip, betrayal, disappointment, regret, brokenness, hurt, and sin.

It is exciting to envision friendship free not only of these many vices but also of the limitations of time itself. As Joni Eareckson Tada observes, "Friendship initiated on earth barely has time to get started; we only scratch its surface in the few short years we reside on earth. Its greater and richer dimension will unfold in heaven."[1] Consequently, she looks forward with great anticipation to the restored and perfected friendships she will enjoy in eternity. Joni is right. We surely will experience unimaginably enriched friendships because we will be fully sanctified and will at last have time and opportunity to deepen our relationships with others to unimaginable depths of intimacy.

Given that we will have an eternity to develop the *quality* of our friendships, will we likewise have an eternity to develop the *quantity* of our friendships? And to take that to an extreme, will we one day enjoy friendship to the *same degree* with all people? Or will it be in heaven as it is now, that we will find ourselves naturally gravitating toward deeper relationships with some people rather than with others? We will explore this question further in dialogue with philosopher Bennett Helm's essay on friendship in the *Stanford Encyclopedia of Philosophy*.

What Makes a Friend?

In his essay, Helm defines friendship as "a distinctively personal relationship that is grounded in a concern on the part of each friend for the welfare of the other, for the other's sake, and that involves some degree of intimacy."[2] In his summary of the philosophical literature, Helm identifies three commonly agreed-on hallmarks of friendship.

To begin with, Helm observes that philosophers writing on friendship are in broad agreement that friendship is marked by *caring*: "Friends must be moved by what happens to their friends to feel the appropriate emotions: joy in their friends' successes, frustration and disappointment in their friends' failures."[3] A friend is a person who is especially invested in the life of the other.

The second criterion is *intimacy*: friends share a closeness of relationship that is not shared with other people. There are various competing conceptions of intimacy in the present age, but not all of them are consistent with friendship in a perfected, heavenly state. For example, some philosophers define intimacy in terms of trust.

This may be a good marker for friendship now, but when everyone is perfectly sinless, it will be possible to trust everyone fully. Yet it won't follow from this that everyone is an equally good friend.

Other philosophers identify friendship with the intimacy of self-disclosure; that is, the willingness to share aspects of yourself with others. This too seems problematic as a marker of friendship in heaven, since the main reason people withhold information from others now is because of shame or embarrassment. But surely we can have no secrets of this type in heaven. In the heavenly state there will no longer be a need to hide from or extend trust to others: "For now we see only a reflection as in a mirror; then we shall see face to face. Now I know in part; then I shall know fully, even as I am fully known" (1 Cor. 13:12). However we end up defining the intimacy of friendship in eternity, it likely will look somewhat different from how intimacy appears in our fallen world.

Finally, friends enjoy *engaging in shared activities*. These might include things like going hiking, eating dinner, rebuilding a motorcycle engine, or playing baseball.

These three hallmarks provide a helpful overview of the main components of friendship. To be a friend with another is to share with that person a special degree of caring, intimacy, and activity not shared with others. So our question can be restated like this: Will we share the same degree of friendship (of caring, intimacy, and shared activities) with all the people in heaven?

Jesus and His Friends

We can begin by considering the friendships Jesus cultivated during his first earthly sojourn. Not only did he choose twelve apostles out of the crowds of disciples, but he also appears to have chosen an inner circle from that group (consisting of Peter, James, and John) whom he took with him on special occasions, such as to the Mount of Transfiguration (Matt. 17:1). Perhaps most striking, five times the Gospel of John refers to "the disciple whom Jesus loved." That phrase seems to be an unapologetic reference to a special relationship Jesus shared with John but not the other apostles. If Jesus had a range of friendships with varying degrees of intimacy, why wouldn't we expect to have something similar in heaven?

It may be possible for Jesus in heaven to retain equal caring and intimacy with all people in virtue of his omnipresence. It may even be possible for him to calibrate his level of shared activities with all people to ensure that he is best friends with all. But the question isn't whether it is *possible* for Jesus to be equally good friends with all people in eternity. The question, rather, is whether he would *in fact* be equally good friends with all people. He will certainly be the same mediator to God the Father for us all. But couldn't the man Jesus still find in eternity that he naturally develops more intimate relationships with some people (e.g., John the beloved apostle) than others (e.g., me)?

The Rest of Us and Our Friends

Even if Jesus does share the same level of friendship with all people in eternity, that doesn't necessarily mean that we will. After all, it is a safe bet that he will be able to do things as divine that we will not, and juggling a few billion friendships is a great example. Even if we pessimistically lowball our estimate of the number in heaven to 100 million, it still staggers the imagination to think that any human other than Jesus could maintain the same degree of caring, intimacy, and shared activity with this number of people.

So both for the christological precedent and in recognition of the finitude of our own human nature, it seems very likely that in eternity human beings will naturally cultivate friendships with a select group of people. Perhaps the key is to recognize that the set of one's friends is an *open* set. Unlike the closed cliques of this life, we will always be open to the discovery of shared interests and perspective with new people for eternity. The idea of having special friends in heaven is *not* a matter of excluding those who are not in our inner circle but rather a recognition of the joys of being in relationship with others. All those friendships, even as they are at varying degrees of development, will be healed of the various ills that infect friendship now.

It has been said that old friends are the best friends. Whether or not this is true, in heaven we will discover that resurrected and glorified friends are the very best of all.

HEAVENLY QUESTIONS

1. Do you look forward more to making new friends in heaven or to deepening friendships that you already enjoy?

2. If you could be friends with any famous person in the Bible or church history, who would it be? (By the way, you can't choose Jesus.)
3. Do you think Jesus will have an inner circle of friends in eternity? If so, do you think you'll be among them?

Question 17

Will We Find Intelligent Aliens There?

With over 100 billion galaxies, what are the chances that we are the only intelligent life? While people love to speculate on this question, ultimately it can only be answered by knowing the mind of the Creator, and that is an insight to which we are not privy. But in the interim we can reflect on what it could mean to find intelligent aliens in creation—for time and eternity.

It may be the most memorable scene in a very memorable film. Scientist Ellie Arroway (Jodie Foster) is relaxing on the hood of her car out in the desert in the middle of an array of radio telescopes. Arroway is a scientist working with SETI (Search for Extraterrestrial Intelligence)—not the most exciting or glamorous job. Every day she bides her time analyzing data coming in from the several radio telescopes that are forever scanning deep space for signals of intelligence. Nothing much ever happens.

But this day is different. As the sun sets, Arroway begins to doze as she listens through headphones to the radio static coming in from deep space. And then suddenly she hears an inexplicable, strong pulse coming from the Vega system. She leaps up and in moments is in the car racing down the road toward the central station and calling out for her two fellow workers to track the signal—and things are never the same again.

The scene comes from *Contact*, a 1997 film based on a 1982 novel by Carl Sagan. Both the book and film explore the fascinating prospect of first contact with an alien civilization. The film was popular with audiences and critics alike for its sober and philosophical portrayal of first contact. The late esteemed film critic Roger Ebert concludes his review of the film like this:

> When I look up at the sky through a telescope, when I follow the landing of the research vehicle on Mars, when I read about cosmology, I brush against transcendence. The universe is so large and old and beautiful, and our life as an intelligent species is so brief, that all our knowledge is like a tiny hint surrounded by a void. Has another race been around longer and learned more? Where are they? We have been listening for only a few decades. Space and time are so vast. A signal's chances of reaching us at the right time and place are so remote they make a message in a bottle look reliable. But if one came. . . .[1]

The ellipsis at the end of the passage is what captures my attention. How do we fill in the ellipsis? What would it mean to make first contact with extraterrestrial intelligence (ETI)?

Would ETI Be a Problem for Christianity?

Many Christians have viewed the idea of ETI with suspicion. They fear that the proper way to fill in Ebert's ellipsis is to add "it would spell trouble for Christianity." This assumption is shared by many non-Christians like physicist Paul Davies. He writes:

> The difficulties are particularly acute for Christianity, which postulates that Jesus Christ was God incarnate whose mission was to provide salvation for man on Earth. The prospect of a host of "alien Christs" systematically visiting every inhabited planet in the physical form of the local creatures has a rather absurd aspect. Yet how otherwise are the aliens to be saved?[2]

So the problem, as Davies sees it, is that Christianity would require the "absurdity" of multiple incarnations to save alien species.

When you scratch beneath the surface, much of the absurdity that people may feel about the issue seems to trace to the so-called

Copernican principle, which states simply that *the earth does not occupy a privileged or special place in the cosmos*. Ever since the sixteenth-century astronomer Nicolas Copernicus forwarded the thesis that the earth is not the fixed center of the universe (in contrast to the Ptolemaic cosmology of the time), repeated discoveries have challenged the uniqueness of human beings and our planet in the cosmos. The more *average* our planet (and sun, solar system, and galaxy) appears, the more difficult it is for some people to believe that human beings have a special place in creation and are made in the image of God. Once people adopt this perspective, it is often assumed that the discovery of an ETI civilization would provide the final nail in the coffin of human uniqueness, thereby definitively undermining the credibility of Christianity.

With these kinds of assumptions, it is no surprise that many Christians today view ETI as a threat to their faith. The antagonism is evident when Christians feel compelled to launch a preemptive strike against the Copernican principle by arguing against the statistical possibility of life arising elsewhere in the universe.[3] But it is a mistake to try to argue that the development of ETI elsewhere in the universe is statistically unlikely, given that for a theist, the statistics depend on our knowing God's intentions, and we simply are not privy to God's thoughts regarding life elsewhere in the cosmos.

Are Alien Incarnations Possible? Are They Necessary?

Let's turn back to Paul Davies's question. If there are aliens, then how are they to be saved? The question assumes that aliens *need* to be saved, which in turn assumes that ETI are fallen. But we can't simply assume this since we already know of at least *one* unfallen class of superintelligent agents in the universe: we call them *angels*. Consequently, we should in principle be open to the possibility that there are more.[4]

If ETI exists and they *are* fallen, then Davies's question becomes important. His proposed answer is that every fallen civilization would require its own incarnation—an *alien Christ*—to save it. Interestingly, this response was anticipated in Christian rock pioneer Larry Norman's 1975 song "UFO" in which he sang that if other planets exist then Jesus has already visited them and died to redeem their species.[5] In fact, the idea of multiple incarnations is nothing new. It turns out that theologians have been reflecting on the possibility of ETI, and multiple incarnations, for *centuries*.[6] And many theologians have concluded that the existence of ETI is fully consonant with their Christian convictions: if God chooses to create and redeem other creatures, it surely is his right to do so.

There are two important problems with the idea of multiple incarnations, however. The first problem concerns whether another incarnation would be necessary. The assumption of the New Testament is that Christ's incarnation and atonement are cosmic in redemptive scope. When one reads the sweeping extent of Christ's work in a passage like Colossians 1:20, there is little doubt that Paul would have believed that Christ's sacrifice touches alien civilizations in the outer reaches of the known universe, had he believed any existed.

The second problem centers on whether multiple incarnations are even *possible*. This problem will take a bit more work to unpack, so your patience is appreciated. In order to see the problem, we will have to draw on two principles: the transitivity of identity and the indiscernibility of identicals.

Let's begin with the *transitivity of identity*. This principle establishes that identity is a transitive relation; it can be stated like this: if A = B and B = C then A = C. This reasoning is operative in the following three-step argument:

1. (A) Dave's Ferrari is (B) the Ferrari parked in the driveway.
2. (B) The Ferrari parked in the driveway is (C) the Ferrari that won a blue ribbon at Pebble Beach.
3. Therefore, (A) Dave's Ferrari is (C) the Ferrari that won a blue ribbon at Pebble Beach.

This makes good sense, right? Now let's consider how the transitivity of identity would apply to an alien incarnation. Imagine a fallen species called the Quar-lawah that lives on planet X-45. In order to save this fallen race, God the Son incarnated on X-45 as an alien life-form named Eweta at the same time he incarnated on earth as Jesus. The transitivity of identity applies to this case as surely as it does to Dave's Ferrari:

1. (A) Eweta is (B) God the Son.
2. (B) God the Son is (C) Jesus.
3. Therefore, (A) Eweta is (C) Jesus.

In the same way that Dave's Ferrari is identical to the Ferrari that won a blue ribbon at Pebble Beach, so it follows that Eweta is identical to Jesus.

Now we turn to the second principle called the *indiscernibility of identicals*. According to this principle, if two things are identical to each other, then they will be indiscernible from each other (i.e., they will share all the same properties). Obviously, if Dave's Ferrari is identical to the Ferrari that won the blue ribbon at Pebble Beach, then it is *indiscernible* from the Ferrari that won a blue ribbon at Pebble Beach. Thus, if Dave's Ferrari presently has a flat tire, then the Ferrari that won a blue ribbon at Pebble Beach must have a flat tire since they are the same car.

With that in mind, all we need to do to test the claim that Jesus is Eweta is to compare their properties. If they have different properties, then they cannot be the same identical person. And obviously, they do have very different properties. Jesus is 5 feet 8 inches tall (or thereabouts) with piercing hazel eyes, brown shoulder-length hair, and a thick beard. By contrast, Eweta has one large purple eye, thick slimy green skin, and twelve tentacles that enable him (or her?) to locomote like an octopus on land. Given that Eweta and Jesus are radically distinct, it follows that they must be different entities. Since Christians believe that God the Son is Jesus, we must reject the claim that God the Son can be any other incarnate being, including Eweta.

While this kind of reasoning makes me skeptical of multiple incarnations, nonetheless, it would be foolhardy for me to think I've provided the last word on the subject, not least because the indiscernibility of identicals, and its sister principle the identity of indiscernibles, have seen their share of philosophical controversy. With that caveat in mind, in the next section we will consider the possibility of aliens in heaven.

ETI in a Heavenly Eternity

If human beings are not alone in the universe, then there is a reasonable chance that we will not be alone in heaven either. And if we are not alone, then there is a possibility that we may discover ETI while exploring the redeemed universe. It may be that an ETI species is unfallen like the angels, but what if it is fallen like us? How then could it have been redeemed into heaven?

What if my argument based on the indiscernibility of identicals is wrong and God the Son did incarnate as an alien life-form for that species while simultaneously incarnating as Jesus? This opens up the mind-bending idea that heaven may offer the possibility to commune with God the Son not only as the eternally incarnate Jesus but also as the eternally incarnate green, octopus-like creature named Eweta, and who knows what else.

Another scenario proposes that God the Son became Jesus only for his earthly sojourn and then left his humanity behind to incarnate into other alien life-forms. This scenario may be logically possible, but it does demand that Christians surrender the classic Christian teaching that the incarnation represents an eternal change in God the Son. (See the discussion on the eternal humanity of Christ in chapter 15.)

But what if I am right and the incarnation of Jesus is the only one in the universe? Does that mean the alien civilization is lost barring our gospel proclamation to it? It need not be. Christians have long debated the salvation of human beings who have never heard the gospel, and those discussions would be applicable to aliens who have never heard the gospel.

The idea that you need to have heard and accepted a gospel presentation to be saved by Jesus is called *exclusivism*. While there are many Christians who are exclusivists, other Christians take an inclusivist position. That is, they believe that some people may be saved by Jesus even if they haven't heard and accepted the gospel. If it is possible that people can be saved without having heard the gospel, perhaps it is possible for aliens as well.[7]

Exclusivism and inclusivism offer different possibilities for how ETI may end up in heaven. We can begin by considering an exclusivist account of alien salvation. This position would declare that aliens must hear the gospel before they can be saved by it. But if they have not had an opportunity to hear it in this life, then when can they hear it? Many theologians have speculated that human beings who don't have a chance to hear the gospel in this life may have an opportunity to do so in the next.[8] If we extend that second chance idea to cover alien civilizations, then it is possible that one of the tasks of the redeemed in eternity will be to proclaim the gospel to alien civilizations who did not have an opportunity on this side of eternity to hear and accept the gospel.[9]

Things look a bit different in the inclusivist scenario. In this case, aliens may be saved by Jesus while never having heard the gospel.

Based on that salvation, they could be resurrected into God's redeemed creation, only to discover after the fact that it was Jesus who saved them. Perhaps they will only learn of the Jesus who saves them when human beings establish first contact with them in God's restored creation. Yes, this is certainly speculative, but for all we know it is possible.

Both scenarios lead to an exciting possibility that Christians in heaven may have as one of their tasks going out into the universe to proclaim to alien civilizations the one who has saved them. Consider the following illustration:

> There is a village named Terra nestled near the head of a great valley. One day massive flood waters come rolling down from the mountains and threaten to wipe out Terra altogether. But before the water reaches the village, the king of Terra orders that one of the walls of his great palace be knocked into the river to create a dam, which stops the flood waters and saves the village. The villagers know that the benevolent king saved them, and they give thanks to him accordingly.
>
> Then one day some of the villagers decide to explore farther down the valley. While they do not know if there are any other villages, they determine that if there are, they will make those villagers aware of how the actions of the king of Terra saved all the villages downstream from certain doom.

Christians living in a redeemed universe could find themselves in a similar situation. They may discover that the universe is in fact teeming with intelligent civilizations—creatures who were, unbeknownst to them, saved by the work of Jesus. And thus redeemed humans may find themselves departing on special missions of evangelistic proclamation to acquaint the innumerable civilizations of the vast cosmos with the God who has saved them. Given the unimaginably fantastic size of the universe and the potential for untold numbers of civilizations thriving among the stars, this could provide a task that would take an eternity.

Heavenly Questions

1. Do you find the idea of first contact with ETI exciting or unnerving? Or does it just strike you as too "Hollywood" to take seriously?

2. If ETI do exist, do you think they must be fallen? If so, how do you think they might be redeemed?

3. What role do you think ETI could play in eternity? Does this discussion have any practical relevance for the Christian life now?

Will We Still Have Free Will?

The tension between heaven and free will is a perennial one. While we presently have the freedom to choose evil, in eternity we will only be able to choose the good. But if we can only choose the good, can we be truly free?

Did you ever have a friend whom your parents labeled a "bad influence"? You know what I mean—the guy who was always getting you into trouble. One minute he'd suggest that you throw snowballs at cars. The next minute he'd have you smashing bottles on the railroad tracks, and later he'd get you to steal gum from the convenience store. Eventually you'd get caught for your shenanigans, and a swift punishment followed. But not long after you were sent to your room to contemplate the depth of your indiscretions, you'd hear a gentle knock on your window pane. And there was your friend with a mischievous grin, inviting you out for more trouble.

Your parents needn't have worried too much. As you grew up, you found you were outgrowing your wayward friend's troublemaking ways. Eventually the prospect of petty theft and vandalism no longer held the appeal it once did. You began to realize that it was time to get serious about life, to grow up and do the right thing. You were drifting apart, and before you knew it, you had left your old friend behind. And looking back, you realized that you didn't even miss him. You now saw him as nothing but trouble.

In our present fallen state, free will is like that friend who keeps getting us into trouble. But that raises a problem, for if it is impossible to sin in heaven, then does that mean we will have to give up our free will to go there? Some theologians believe so. Clark Pinnock observes that while "we are free to enter into union with God, . . . it may be that in heaven, the purpose of our probation having been fulfilled, *freedom may be withdrawn.*"[1] This is a significant problem, for people generally consider their freedom to be an important value that they do not surrender lightly. Is there a way out of this dilemma? Is it possible to have our free will and heaven too?

Pinnock's dilemma clearly presupposes that to be free is to be able to sin. While this is a common assumption,[2] I think it is clearly false. And I will aim to establish its falsity with respect to the two basic theories of free action.

Freedom and Determination

At this point we need to consider two different views of free will. The crucial issue that separates these two positions is whether free will is understood to be compatible with determinism. According to determinism, for every event that occurs there are prior conditions that necessitated the occurrence of that event. Thus, the question is whether one could be free to do an action that is determined by prior conditions.

Philosophers agree that a free action first requires that the actor choose to do the act because he *wants* to. But philosophers disagree on whether free will is compatible with determinism. *Compatibilists* believe that free action is compatible with determinism. *Incompatibilists* disagree, stating that if an act is determined by prior causes, then it cannot be free. Thus, they believe that free will is incompatible with determinism.

We can explore the difference between the two views by focusing on a specific case. Say, for example, that you clap your hands when "Shine Jesus Shine" is played during a church service. Were you free to clap your hands? The incompatibilist will make the answer dependent on whether there were prior factors that determined that you would clap your hands. It may be that every time you hear "Shine Jesus Shine," you simply *must* clap. If that is true, then according to the incompatibilist, you were not really free to clap. The compatibilist disagrees, countering that even if you were determined to clap your hands, you could still be free to do it as long as you *wanted* to do it.

It follows that the compatibilist has no problem with free will in heaven because being determined to do good is compatible with freely doing good. Consequently, the compatibilist can avoid Pinnock's dilemma by saying that in heaven we will be perfectly sanctified and thus will be determined to do only the good. But because we will *want* to do only the good, we will be free to do it.

A Transformation of Taste

What about those who are incompatibilists, like Pinnock? Is incompatibilist free will possible in heaven if we are unable to do evil? The short answer is yes. We can be undetermined and free even if we can only make good choices. We can illumine the point by shifting to a culinary illustration.

Imagine a man named Buzz who has a taste for junk food but who lacks a general appreciation for healthy gourmet food. If you offer Buzz the following meals, he will respond like this:

Unhealthy Big Mac: possibly yes

Healthy poached salmon: possibly yes

Healthy barley and birch soup: definitely no

Consequently, Buzz is presently in a place where he will sometimes freely choose a good meal (e.g., poached salmon) and sometimes choose a bad meal (e.g., Big Mac). But there are some good meals he will never choose (e.g., barley and birch soup).

Then Buzz meets Edith, a vivacious foodie who is very interested in the perfect melding of flavor, presentation, and nutrition. Slowly but surely Edith brings about a transformation in Buzz's perception of various foods. She introduces him to an intoxicating range of gastronomic possibilities, reveals to him the importance of preparation and presentation, and invites him to discover all sorts of previously unimagined ingredients and flavor combinations.

Their culinary journey together culminates with an evening at Noma, an establishment in Copenhagen that has been lauded as the world's best restaurant.[3] There is no Big Mac on the menu. But by this time, even if there were, Buzz *would not* order it because he has been transformed. Based on all he now knows and has experienced of food, he will never again order a Big Mac. Thus, things now look like this:

Unhealthy Big Mac: definitely no
Healthy poached salmon: possibly yes
Healthy barley and birch soup: possibly yes

Has Buzz lost his free will? Of course not. While some foods have been lost to his palette, others have been opened up. Scanning the menu at Noma, he can now see that the barley and birch soup looks wonderful, as do dozens of other extraordinary creations that Buzz would never have considered before meeting Edith. While he has lost the ability to make bad culinary choices, Buzz's transformed perspective has opened up vast new culinary horizons, and, given that those are objectively better choices, that change has made him freer than ever. With the bad choices definitively removed from his palate like chaff that has been burned away, only excellent culinary choices remain on his horizon. Yes, he's determined by his culinary formation to choose from among those excellent choices, but he's still free to choose which of those many excellent choices he'll have.

The gastronomic metaphor is a fitting one given that one of the central images of the new creation is a meal of unparalleled quality. Isaiah 25:6 promises a banquet to put all the Michelin three-star restaurants in the world to shame: "On this mountain the Lord Almighty will prepare a feast of rich food for all peoples, a banquet of aged wine—the best of meats and the finest of wines."

Unfortunately, right now with our fallen moral tastes, we are as likely to quaff a glass of Two Buck Chuck from the grocery store as a glass of the finest French merlot.[4] When it comes to the "best of meats," we're as likely to choose a Big Mac as a filet mignon. And where rich food is concerned, we're just as likely to opt for a Twinkie as a glass of sparkling shiraz jelly complemented with frosted grapes. One day, however, our tastes will be transformed as heaven reveals to us an infinite horizon of culinary delicacies. We will have no desire to choose evil but will have an infinite range of good choices.

The Bad Influence Becomes Good

From here we can turn back to our opening illustration of the wayward friend. As the original story goes, we gradually drift away from our friend and go our separate way while he remains locked in perpetual adolescence. Say good-bye to free will.

The picture of heaven explored by our culinary illustration suggests a very different possibility. In this telling, we don't grow out of our friend. Rather, he grows along with us. As we move to a point of rejecting petty theft and vandalism, so does he. Together we become more mature, gradually leaving behind a life of sinful activities. And if our friend matures along with us, then there is never a need to give him up. When we come to the banquet, we do so *with* our free will and open to the infinite enjoyments of the meal of a lifetime—for eternity.

HEAVENLY QUESTIONS

1. What do you think it means to be free, and why is freedom so important?

2. Do you think people can be free to do good if they cannot also choose to do evil?

3. Do you think God is free? What does it mean for God to be free?

Part 5

Hell

The heavenly equation may illumine the nature of heaven and earth, but can it hope to bring light to the impossibly difficult doctrine of hell? In the final two chapters we will consider whether glorified persons can find joy in those suffering in hell and whether it is proper for us to hope that hell may one day be emptied.

Question 19

If My Child Goes to Hell, Will I Know and Will I Care?

How can people exist redeemed in heavenly bliss while their loved ones are suffering unimaginable torment in hell? Christians have often sought to deal with this problem by suggesting that the redeemed will be unaware of the suffering of the damned. However, many scriptural passages suggest that far from being unaware, the redeemed will actually rejoice in the damnation of others. But how can that be?

There is probably no question more agonizing for a Christian than this: How can I be happy in heaven with a loved one in hell? While this is a deeply emotional question, it is also a logical one rooted in the apparent inconsistency between the following three propositions:

1. In heaven the redeemed will be maximally happy.
2. In heaven the redeemed will be maximally loving.
3. In heaven the redeemed will be aware of the suffering of the damned in hell.

The problem arises when we ask how maximally loving people could possibly be *happy* knowing that a portion of God's creatures are suffering unimaginably in hell. On the face of it, that sounds about as implausible as maximally loving parents carrying on serenely with a Mediterranean vacation while some of their children are being tortured in a Turkish prison. It just doesn't compute.

Since rejecting proposition 1 isn't a serious option (we surely will be maximally happy in heaven), we'll have to reevaluate our other two propositions. These days the most popular solution is to reject the third proposition. With the maxim "ignorance is bliss" echoing in the background, it is popular to claim that people in heaven will be completely unaware of those suffering in hell. Perhaps one may even find a friendly proof text in Isaiah 65:17: "The former things will not be remembered, nor will they come to mind."

While the desire to maintain the bliss of heaven provides a strong motivation for rejecting proposition 3, that resolution still faces severe problems. We can illumine those problems by considering why many theologians throughout church history have instead rejected proposition 2. More specifically, they have denied that the redeemed will love the damned or be saddened by their suffering. Indeed, they have argued that the redeemed will actually *delight* in the suffering of the damned.

The Joys of Hell?

Surprising though it may seem, the position of denying love and compassion toward the damned is well represented in church history. Consider the following passage from Tertullian, a theologian of the early third century, in which he anticipates with jaw-dropping candor the time when he will rejoice in the damnation of the church's persecutors:

> You are fond of spectacles; expect the greatest of all spectacles, the last and eternal judgment of the universe. How shall I admire, how laugh, how rejoice, how exult, when I behold so many proud monarchs, and fancied gods, groaning in the lowest abyss of darkness; so many magistrates who persecuted the name of the Lord, liquefying in fiercer flames than they ever kindled against the Christians; so many sage philosophers blushing in red hot flames with their deluded scholars; so many celebrated poets trembling before the tribunal, not of Minos, but of Christ; so many tragedians more tuneful in the expression of their own sufferings; so many dancers writhing in the flames.[1]

That's pretty intense stuff. Not only does Tertullian deny that the saved will be compassionate toward the damned, he actually goes on to affirm that they will *laugh* as the wicked do the damnation dance in Gehenna's flames. This takes fire-and-brimstone preaching to a whole new level!

It is tempting to dismiss Tertullian as an antisocial misanthrope who simply hadn't read his Bible enough. After all, everybody knows that the biblical God is maximally "compassionate and gracious, slow to anger, abounding in love" (Ps. 103:8). He takes no pleasure in the death of the wicked (Ezek. 18:23) but desires that all be saved (1 Tim. 2:4). If God is perfectly loving and compassionate, then surely perfectly redeemed human beings will be as well.

Unfortunately, Tertullian's shocking opinion cannot be dismissed so easily. The problem is that there are many biblical texts that support the idea that both God and his servants *will* exult in the destruction of the wicked. Just consider the imprecatory (cursing) psalms as an example. In some of these passages the psalmist declares that the Lord and his righteous followers will laugh at the demise of the wicked (e.g. Ps. 37:13; 56:2). Even more shocking, the psalmist also hopes that the wicked will not repent and seek salvation (Ps. 69:23–24, 28).

Lest you think that those sentiments are restricted to a more brutish Old Testament era, be advised that a similar theme can be found in the New Testament, most perspicuously in the book of Revelation. To begin with, the martyrs cry out to God to avenge their blood (Rev. 6:10)—a plea that clearly implies the desire to see their persecutors get their comeuppance. Moreover, when the damned are sent to eternal agony, the Lamb and his angels will have front-row seats to their suffering (Rev. 14:10–11). This is clearly not the picture of Jesus wringing his hands in distress over the lost sheep. Consequently, when judgment is finally exercised and God's enemies are defeated, there will be no sadness or regret but only praise: "Hallelujah! The smoke from her goes up for ever and ever" (Rev. 19:3).

Given the prevalence of this biblical theme, it should come as no surprise that many theologians have followed Tertullian in rejecting proposition 2. For example, Thomas Aquinas makes three points in his *Summa Theologiae* concerning "the relation of the saints toward the damned." He begins by claiming that the saints will see the suffering of the damned because it will deepen their appreciation for heaven.[2] Next, he denies that the elect will pity the damned in any way, because that would be inconsistent with their state of happiness.

And finally, he claims that the suffering of the damned will be a cause for rejoicing among the saints, not out of malice but rather as a demonstration of divine justice.[3]

On the Idea of *Schadenfreude*

The idea that the saints will rejoice in the suffering of the damned calls to mind the German concept of *Schadenfreude*, which is the idea of finding joy or satisfaction in the misfortune or misery of others. You may not have heard the word before, but I'm sure you are familiar with the concept. Let me give you an example:

When I was seven years old, I went to the corner store with my brother and two friends. Shortly after we arrived, a boy of twelve or thirteen started picking on us. Immediately my friend Darren, the youngest in a family of three boys, went to the pay phone and called his big brother Stu for help. Within five minutes Stu came barreling into the parking lot in his old Ford pickup. At that point I called out to our tormenter, "*Now* you're going to get it, *kid*!" Even as the bully turned to look at me in surprise and anger, Stu jumped out of the pickup, strode up behind him, and grabbed him roughly by the collar. In the ensuing moments, as I gleefully watched Stu put the bully in his place, I enjoyed my first real experience of *Schadenfreude*. And did it ever feel good!

One finds many examples of *Schadenfreude* in the Bible. Consider, for example, the scene in the book of Esther when the queen bravely informs King Xerxes of Haman's plan to kill the Jews. Xerxes immediately turns on his trusted advisor Haman, leaving the wicked man to plead pathetically to Queen Esther for his life (Esther 7). The narrator does not expect the reader to feel compassion for Haman in this moment. Instead, the narrative sets us up for an emotionally satisfying payoff as this would-be genocidaire faces the ironic fate of being impaled on the very pole on which he had planned to execute the pious Jew Mordecai. Take that, Haman!

Schadenfreude may be familiar to us, but that doesn't mean we're entirely comfortable with it. Whether the case is relatively trivial, like a bully being bullied, or more profound, like a perpetrator of genocide being executed, there seems to be something wrong with taking satisfaction in the misfortune of others. Consequently, many ethicists have concluded that *Schadenfreude* is actually immoral.[4] When it comes to the doctrine of hell, many theologians agree. For example, John Stott writes, "I want to repudiate with all the vehemence of which I am capable the glibness, what almost appears to be the glee, the *Schadenfreude*, with which some Evangelicals speak about hell. It is a horrible sickness of mind or spirit."[5]

So should we reject *Schadenfreude* outright? Before doing so we ought to think more about Aquinas's distinction between a cruel or malicious satisfaction in the punishment of others and that which is rooted in the revelation of God's justice. In his discussion of the topic, philosopher Lars Svendsen endorses this same distinction: "There are two clear reasons for schadenfreude: a general delight in another's suffering or a specific delight in seeing justice done." He then observes, "In my opinion, schadenfreude is an acceptable feeling if it's motivated by justice; that is, *if it's not the suffering itself, but the sense of justice being done, that produces the pleasure.*"[6]

John Portman would agree. In his book on *Schadenfreude* he argues that we need to distinguish mere delight in suffering from delight in seeing justice fulfilled. He writes, "We morally withhold some or all of our compassion for those who suffer if we believe that they have brought their suffering upon themselves." In Portman's view, the morally serious expression of *Schadenfreude* is "an emotional corollary of justice."[7] It is not petty vindictiveness but rather a deep satisfaction at seeing the injustices in the world being set right.

The Real Problem with *Schadenfreude*

I tend to agree with Aquinas, Svendsen, and Portman that there is a morally defensible type of *Schadenfreude*. Consider, for example, the satisfaction in seeing a corrupt ruler being stripped of his power and pulled before the International Court of Justice to account for his crimes. When the demands of justice are met, we find it satisfying, as we should. If we, fallen creatures that we are, can find pleasure in God's justice being exercised on earth, how much more will we, when we are glorified, be able to take full pleasure in his justice exercised in eternity?

The real problem when it comes to hell is not *Schadenfreude* per se. Rather, it is the assumption that satisfaction in the expression of justice will not be intermingled with compassion and sorrow. Consider this illustration: Imagine that there is a vandal plaguing your mobile home park who is smashing the garden gnomes under cover of night. Like everyone else, you long to see the vandal apprehended to receive his just punishment. But when he is arrested, you discover that the culprit is your own son. If, after this revelation, you continue to experience *Schadenfreude* that the guilty party has been arrested, I should admire your commitment to and satisfaction in objective justice. (You do the crime, you do the time!) But if you do not also experience sorrow that your son committed the crime and will have to endure the punishment, I would consider you inexplicably cold and detached. Consequently, whatever pleasure you would experience at the satisfaction of justice ought to be tempered by sorrow, compassion, and regret at your son's actions and the punishment he must bear.

I can see no reason to think this will change at the general resurrection when you are fully conformed to Jesus. At that moment, you could experience a sense of satisfaction that the scales of injustice are at long last being righted. You could be content knowing that each individual in hell will receive a punishment directly commensurate to the crime committed.

The problem comes with the suggestion that you would not also experience deep sadness, even anguish, looking out and seeing loved ones among the hordes of those damned. After all, Jesus—the one to whom you will be completely conformed—anguished over the coming judgment of God's people (Matt. 23:37) and prayed for his persecutors even while on the cross (Luke 23:34). Why wouldn't you experience a similar anguish for your loved ones, and indeed all of the damned? Even if you did experience *Schadenfreude*, wouldn't it be infused with sorrow?

The traditional position says no; heavenly *Schadenfreude* will be pure joy with no sadness, no lament. As we saw, Tertullian suggests it could even involve mirthful laughter as the damned writhe in the flames. Maybe so, but from my present imperfect perspective that suggestion seems impossibly cruel, incomprehensibly detached, and very far from the character of Jesus.

Could You Ever Be Happy to See Your Child Damned?

The best way for us to appreciate the force of this dilemma is to switch from vague generalities to a thick narrative.[8] While the story I tell will illumine the practical problem of *Schadenfreude* not tempered by sorrow, it will also raise broader questions about the nature and justice of hell as traditionally conceived.

Imagine that you have a twenty-five-year-old daughter named Lizzie. She is a wonderful girl, the light of your life, gentle and caring, and very bright. Over the years she has volunteered her time at various charities to help the poor and oppressed. Now she is realizing her dream by studying to be a social worker. Life is good.

Then Lizzie takes you out for coffee and tells you that she simply cannot believe "that Christianity stuff" any longer. Her decision hurts you deeply, but it is clear she has struggled over it. What is more, she arrived at it with more thoughtfulness and integrity than most people you know who sit in the pews every Sunday morning and obligingly recite the Apostles' Creed without a second thought.

While it is difficult for you to hear of Lizzie's decision, you appreciate her honesty, and you know that she has truly wrestled over the issues. Regardless of the nature of her religious convictions (or lack thereof), you will always love her dearly. Whether she calls herself a Christian or not, she remains the same gentle, loving spirit you have always known, and your deep parental bond is unchanged by this difficult news. You assure her that she will always be your little girl, even if she doesn't share your faith.

A few days after Lizzie's painful confession, she is volunteering at a nearby battered women's shelter when the unthinkable happens. The estranged husband of one of the women staying at the shelter arrives and begins pounding on the door. Immediately Lizzie springs into action, leading the terrified young woman to a safe room—with space for only one. Just as Lizzie locks the entry to the safe room, the woman's husband breaks in the front door. "You stupid whore!" he screams at Lizzie. "Where did you hide her?"

"I don't know what you're talking about," Lizzie replies firmly.

Without warning, the intruder pulls out a Ruger semi-automatic and shoots Lizzie in the face, killing her instantly.

Given that Lizzie told you she rejected the gospel, you have reason to believe that she has gone to hell. At that moment, the grief at her loss is unimaginable. But is it possible that when you are resurrected into heavenly glory, fully conformed to the image of God's Son, the grief you now feel will be transformed into joy that God is righteously punishing Lizzie in hell for eternity? Could this really be what it means to become fully like the God revealed in Jesus?

Therein lies the dilemma. If you wouldn't experience deep pain and sadness in heaven at Lizzie's eternal fate, then what does it even mean to be made like Christ? But if you would experience it, what then becomes of heaven?

HEAVENLY QUESTIONS

1. Do you ever take satisfaction in the misfortune of others? Do you think it is ever appropriate to do so?

2. What do you think is the best way to reconcile the bliss of heaven with the agonies of hell? Do you think the saints will be unaware of those in hell? Or do you think the suffering of the damned will enrich the pleasures of the saints?

3. What is your reaction to the Lizzie story? Do you think it is helpful in clarifying the issues? Why or why not?

Should We Hope That Everyone Will Be Saved?

We're not supposed to want anyone to go to hell. So why don't we say that we hope everyone goes to heaven? The reason, presumably, is because we believe that there is simply no possibility that everyone can be saved. But are we sure about that?

Imagine that you're on a cruise ship that has hit a rocky shoal and is sinking. As soon as you feel the lurch and hear the grinding of metal, you immediately make your way to a lifeboat along with a smattering of other passengers. As your lifeboat is being lowered into the water, the massive vessel begins to list dangerously to one side. Despite this fact, scores of people remain on the ship, inexplicably disregarding the warnings as they continue to dance and dine as if everything is fine. While a few people are making their way to the lifeboats and imploring others as they go, it appears that most are not heeding the warnings.

At this moment it would be completely reasonable for you to believe that not everyone will be saved from the ship. But even so, as long as there is the faintest possibility that all may be saved, surely you ought to *hope* that all will be saved.

If Christianity is true, then those who are in Christ are now sitting in the lifeboats watching the sinking ship. The way things look at present, Christians may well believe that not all the passengers will find their way into the lifeboats. But surely Christians ought to *hope* that they will. And they ought to be clear about expressing that hope.

To say that you hope everybody is saved is to say that you hope *universalism* is true. Now I know what you're about to say: "Hold on a minute! Universalism is a heresy, isn't it? And I can't very well hope that a heresy is true!" The fact is that people can mean all kinds of things when they refer to universalism, and some of them probably are heretical. But then people also mean all sorts of things when they refer to Christianity, and some of those things are also heretical. That doesn't mean we stop hoping Christianity is true! Instead, the lesson is that we should be careful to define our terms, whether the label in question is *Christianity* or *universalism* or anything else.

When I say *universalism*, I mean the view that all people will eventually be saved by God through the work of Jesus Christ. That confession is consistent with all the major dogmas of faith including the Trinity, incarnation, atonement, and justification by grace through faith. It is even consistent with affirming the existence of hell after death, so long as hell is understood as the process by which people are purified for heaven (in other words, hell as purgatory). So *hopeful universalism* doesn't mean hoping that a heresy is true. It simply means hoping that everyone will be reconciled to God in Christ. Given that the salvation of all would be such a wonderful outcome, why *shouldn't* we hope that this is true?

The Bible Leaves No Room for Hope—Does It?

This question invites an obvious response: there is no room for hope because *the Bible doesn't leave any room for hope*. For example, in the parable of the sheep and goats, Jesus declares to those on his left, "Depart from me, you who are cursed, into the eternal fire prepared for the devil and his angels" (Matt. 25:41). Could he have been any clearer than that? People *will* go to hell forever, so there is no sense in hoping that they won't.

But that may be too hasty. Let's consider another passage that seems to be eminently clear. In Exodus 33:20 God declares, "You cannot see my face, for no one may see me and live." That seems straightforward enough: nobody can see God and live, period. And yet apparently it isn't that clear because Jesus declared that you *can* see God by looking at *him* (John 14:8–9). What are we to make of this?

Let me suggest that the lesson we should draw is one of *epistemic fallibility*. In other words, we should recognize that we could be wrong about the meaning or significance we ascribe to various biblical texts—even those that seem to be simple and straightforward. If people could be wrong about a *clear* passage like Exodus 33:20, perhaps they could also be wrong in reading *hell passages* like Matthew 25:41.

Please keep in mind that I'm not claiming that we *are* wrong in reading Matthew 25:41 and other hell passages as supporting a doctrine of eternal hell. (Although the complexity of translating the Greek word *aionios*, which is commonly rendered in English as "eternal," certainly allows for that possibility.) Instead, the main point is that we cannot be certain that we're right in this reading. And if there is even a tiny possibility that we could be wrong, we ought to hope that we are, given that being wrong would have such an extraordinary outcome—salvation for all!

Think about it like this. When you buy a ticket in the Mega Millions Lottery, it makes no sense to believe you'll win given the astronomical odds. Even so, the miniscule possibility that you could win is sufficient to ground the *hope* that you'll win. *Low odds may not warrant belief, but they do warrant hope*. Indeed, that's why you bought the ticket in the first place. By the same token, the most miniscule of possibilities is not adequate to ground belief in universalism, but it is adequate to ground the hope.

Our hope can be buoyed further if we take note of the fact that a minority of theologians throughout the history of the church have defended universalism not just as a hope but as a personal conviction. And they've done so based on various biblical, theological, and philosophical arguments.[1] For example, many have pointed out that there are several passages in Scripture that appear at first blush to support universalism, including Romans 5:18; 14:11; 1 Corinthians 15:22; Ephesians 1:10; Philippians 2:11–12; and Colossians 1:20. Typically these passages are interpreted in light of other passages that seem to preclude the possibility of universal salvation (such as Matt. 25:41). But it is at least possible in principle to invert the hermeneutical priority so that the texts that seem to support universal salvation are used as an interpretive grid for those that appear to preclude it.

I am not proposing that we do that here, because I'm not actually aiming to defend universalism. What I am doing, instead, is demonstrating that there is a possibility we could be wrong in our rejection of universalism, and that possibility is sufficient to ground the *hope* that we are wrong, just as a single lottery ticket is sufficient to hope that we win the lottery.

Hopeful Universalism in a Formal Argument

At this point it may be helpful to summarize my case for hopeful universalism in a formal argument:

1. If it is conceivable that all people will be saved by God, then it is right to hope that all people will be saved by God.
2. It is conceivable that all people will be saved by God.
3. Therefore, it is right to hope that all people will be saved by God.

I have already offered a two-pronged defense of the second point. I began with the example of Exodus 33:20 to illustrate how a person can be wrong in assessing the significance of apparently clear passages of Scripture. This in turn grounds the hope that we could be wrong in our interpretation of the hell texts. This hope is strengthened with the observation that many theologians have actually endorsed universalism as a conviction based on biblical, theological, and philosophical argumentation. The very fact that a minority of intelligent Christian scholars have concluded that universalism is true may not be sufficient to persuade us that it is true, but it is at least sufficient to strengthen the hope that it *could* be true.

Given that proposition 2 is well established, everything ultimately hinges on proposition 1. Is it *right* to hope that all are in fact saved by God? I can see two remotely plausible objections to this proposition.

The first objection is derived from the claim of some Calvinists that it is more glorifying to God to save some people and damn others rather than to save them all. Based on this claim, it can be argued that hoping for the salvation of all is tantamount to hoping that God not be perfectly glorified. But since God's glory must take precedence over everything else, including the scope of creaturely salvation, we shouldn't hope for the salvation of all.

This objection is quickly dealt with by simply pointing out that the Calvinist could be wrong in the assumption that God is most fully glorified by damning some people rather than by saving all. Consequently, we ought to hope that this view is wrong and that God can be fully glorified while saving all. In this way we don't have to choose between the hope of universalism and the hope that God will perfectly glorify himself, for we can hope that God is perfectly glorified through the salvation of all.

The second objection is practical in nature because it argues against hopeful universalism based on the allegedly negative consequences that would follow from voicing that hope. In short, the claim is that expressing the hope that God may save all could undermine evangelistic efforts since people could be less likely to share the gospel if they believe God may ultimately save all people. Consequently, on this reasoning we ought not express the hope that God will save all—even if we privately maintain it—for fear of undermining evangelistic motivation.

This too is a weak argument for at least two reasons. To begin with, there is no evidence that maintaining a bare hope that all may be saved would weaken evangelistic efforts. That's like claiming that buying a lottery ticket will cause people to stop contributing to their savings accounts.

Further, even if the hope of universalism could weaken evangelism, that is not a reason to reject it. When Paul was discussing the doctrine of salvation in Romans, he recognized that preaching justification by grace could have the effect of undermining individual efforts at sanctification. Indeed, he recognized that people might even use the doctrine as a pretense to justify an increase in sinful activity. But Paul never considered this danger a reason to remain silent about justification by grace, still less to reject it. Instead, he took direct aim at those who would use the doctrine to defend a lax approach to sanctification (see Rom. 6:1–2).

A similar response is appropriate to anyone who would use the hope of universalism as a pretense not to evangelize. It can be put like this: "What shall we say, then? Shall we no longer do evangelism based on the hope that God might save all? By no means! Christ sent us into all the world to make disciples; how can we refuse to share his glorious gospel?"

Three Benefits of Hopeful Universalism

In closing, I'd like to note three very practical benefits that come with being a hopeful universalist. The first point is an emphasis on *grace.* It is a well-established fact that people tend to be much more forgiving of the sins they commit themselves than of the sins of others (see Matt. 18:21–35). As film critic Roger Ebert observed in his review of *The Woodsman*, a film about a pedophile attempting to reintegrate into society, "We are quick to forgive our own trespasses, slower to forgive those of others. The challenge of a moral life is to do nothing that needs forgiveness. In that sense, we're all out on parole."[2] Indeed we are. And that's one of the strengths of hopeful universalism. By committing to hope for the salvation of all, we are hoping for the salvation of the worst murderers, rapists, and pedophiles. That is a very practical and challenging way to embody a spirit of grace.

Second, hopeful universalism provides a pressure valve for those of us who cannot bear the thought of eternal damnation. Frankly, it is disturbing to see how many Christians are complacent, even comfortable, about the prospect of potentially millions of people suffering in hell for eternity. Seriously contemplating the possibility of hell should absolutely horrify us. As John Stott observes, "Emotionally, I find the concept intolerable and do not understand how people can live with it without either cauterising their feelings or cracking under the strain."[3] Stott eased the strain by embracing annihilationism, the doctrine that the damned will be destroyed at the general resurrection. Reiterating the hope for universal salvation would provide another way. So when the pressure of hell is too much, we can channel our anguish into hopeful prayers for the salvation of all.

Finally, hopeful universalism places hope at the center of the Christian life, which is right where it belongs. It reminds us that too often we've been pessimists who have prematurely concluded that God cannot possibly redeem a particular situation, whether that situation is a broken marriage, a lost job, or a fallen world. And time and again God has proven that pessimism wrong. After a while you'd think we'd become a bit more circumspect over making sweeping judgments about how God will act and what he can and cannot redeem. Hopeful universalism roots itself in that coming day when Christ will "reconcile to himself all things, whether things on earth or things in heaven, by making peace through his blood, shed on the cross" (Col. 1:20).

Amen.

Come, Lord Jesus.

HEAVENLY QUESTIONS

1. What is your view of hell? How many people do you think will end up there?
2. Do you think it is possible that those in hell can be redeemed?
3. Do you think it is right to hope for the salvation of all? Do you agree that hopeful universalism could undermine the will to evangelize?

Afterword

Waiting for the Dream Car

Ever since he was a little boy, his parents had been promising that they would give him a beautiful car to drive when he turned sixteen. And ever since he was a little boy, he had planned to park it in the barn where it was warm and dry.

Only first his dad would have to get rid of the old car sitting in the barn. He didn't know what it was, but it had been sitting under a tarp for as long as he could remember. He couldn't wait for his dad to haul it off to the dump to make way for his dream car.

Ah, the dream car that so often drove its way into his thoughts. Every time his dad took him into town to buy farm supplies, he spent a few minutes lingering at the car dealership, looking at all the bright, shiny automobiles, imagining which one would one day be his.

But when would the day come? When would his new car arrive? And when would Dad get rid of that old car under the tarp to make way for his dream machine?

Then late one evening in early summer with his birthday just a few months away, he heard another sound intermingled with the incessant chirp of the crickets. It sounded like power tools . . . a drill . . . a hammer. What was going on? He peered out into the darkness and could see nothing but the canopy of stars sparkling fiercely over the summer prairie.

And then he noticed it. A light was on in the barn.

He walked out into the warm night air, down the dirt path, and curiously poked his head into the barn door. Immediately he was hit with the earthy aroma of dung and hay.

Then he saw the tarp, rolled up and left against the door. Instantly he was filled with excitement. Was Dad finally getting rid of that old car? Anticipation filled his heart.

At that moment he looked up and saw illuminated by the light of the barn one of the most recognizable sports cars in automotive history. He could identify it right away from the stack of classic car magazines in his bedroom. It was a Corvette, and not just any Corvette. This was the coveted 1963 with a split window, aluminum knock-off wheels, candy apple red paint, and a 327 V8.

That was the car that was underneath the tarp all those years? He stood there stunned.

At that moment his father looked up from where he was working, leaning over the front fender, his hands deep in the engine bay. He made eye contact with his son and smiled broadly.

Then he held out a socket wrench to the boy. "Come on, son," he said. "We have some work to do to get your car ready."

Acknowledgments

Thanks to my agent, Janet Kobobel Grant of Books & Such Literary Agency, for suggesting that I write a book on heaven and then providing invaluable input at every step on the journey. Thanks as well to Robert Hosack, executive editor at Baker Books, and to the whole team at Baker: your enthusiasm for and commitment to this project has been a wonderful encouragement. Finally, thanks as always go to my family—my wife, Jasper (Rae Kyung), and daughter, Jamie—who provide every day the ideal familial backdrop to anticipate the time when God's kingdom comes in its fullness.

Notes

A Most Heavenly Equation

1. David Bodanis, $E = mc^2$: A Biography of the World's Most Famous Equation (New York: Berkley, 2001), 192–93.

2. Margery Williams, The Velveteen Rabbit (repr. New York: Delacorte, 1991; 1922), 5.

Question 1: Where Is Heaven Now?

1. For a fuller discussion of this issue see Randal Rauser, Faith Lacking Understanding: Theology through a Glass Darkly (Carlisle, UK: Paternoster, 2008), chap. 6.

2. For the origins of the hoax, see "Not Frozen Over: Hell Found under Siberia: Screams Scare Scientists," Biblical Archaeology Review 16, no. 6 (1990): 6.

3. See "The Well to Hell," in Jan Harold Brunvand, Encyclopedia of Urban Legends (New York: Norton, 2001), 476–77.

4. See third-century theologian Tertullian in A Treatise on the Soul, chap. 55.

5. Notice I said it has at least one such resident. If Enoch and Elijah both ascended to heaven without dying, then heaven might have two additional physically embodied residents. According to the Catholic dogma of the bodily assumption of Mary, the mother of Jesus could be yet another embodied resident of spiritual heaven.

6. Douglas Farrow, Ascension and Ecclesia: On the Significance of the Doctrine of the Ascension for Ecclesiology and Christian Cosmology (Edinburgh: T & T Clark, 1999), 16.

7. Wayne Grudem, Systematic Theology: An Introduction to Biblical Doctrine (Grand Rapids: Zondervan; Leicester, UK: Inter-Varsity Press, 1994), 617.

8. J. Sidlow Baxter, The Other Side of Death: What the Bible Teaches about Heaven and Hell (Grand Rapids: Kregel, 1997), 216.

9. Ibid., 215.

10. See www.virgingalactic.com.

11. J. Oliver Buswell, "Eschatology," *A Systematic Theology of the Christian Religion*, vol. 4, (Grand Rapids: Zondervan, 1962), 315.

12. For an undergraduate level introduction see Barton Zwiebach, *A First Course in String Theory*, 2nd ed. (Cambridge: Cambridge University Press, 2009).

13. Hugh Ross, *Beyond the Cosmos: The Extra-Dimensionality of God* (Colorado Springs: NavPress, 1996), 46–47.

14. For example, see Robin McKie, "String Theory: Is It Science's Ultimate Dead End?" *The Guardian*, October 7, 2006, www.guardian.co.uk/science/2006/oct/08/research.highereducation.

Question 3: Will the New Earth Include Other Galaxies?

1. Grudem, *Systematic Theology*, 1160–61.

2. Ibid., 1161.

3. Anthony Hoekema, *The Bible and the Future* (Grand Rapids: Eerdmans, 1979), 275.

4. Ibid., 274, emphasis added.

5. Robert W. Messler, Jr., *The Essence of Materials for Engineers* (Mississauga, Ontario, Canada: Jones and Bartlett, 2011), 22.

6. "Singapore Airlines Flight 21," Wikipedia, modified April 22, 2013, http://en.wikipedia.org/wiki/Singapore_Airlines_Flight_21.

7. You can view the image online at the HubbleSite News Release Archive, http://hubblesite.org/newscenter/archive/releases/2007/2007/18/image/a/.

8. Gary Greenberg and Stacy Keach, *A Grain of Sand: Nature's Secret Wonder* (Minneapolis: Voyageur, 2008), 39.

9. Baxter, *Other Side of Death*, 213.

Question 4: What Is God Saving the Universe From?

1. H. G. Wells, *The Time Machine: A Melancholy Satire* (Rockville, MD: Arc Manor Classic Reprints, 2008), 28.

2. Ibid., 87.

3. For a discussion of the heat death of the universe, see Nikos Prantzos, *Our Cosmic Future: Humanity's Fate in the Universe* (Cambridge: Cambridge University Press, 2000).

Question 5: Will We Recognize the Earth When It Is Renewed?

1. Daniel R. Lockwood, "Until We Meet Again," *Christianity Today*, October 2007, 98.

2. C. S. Lewis, *The Last Battle* (New York: Scholastic, 1995), 193.

3. Ibid., 195–96.

4. For further discussion of technology in heaven, see questions 11 and 12.

Question 6: How Old Will We Be—and Will We Get Older?

1. See Thomas Aquinas, *Summa Theologiae*, supplement to III. Q. 81. Art. 1.

2. Thomas Aquinas, *The Aquinas Catechism* (Manchester, NH: Sophia Institute, 2000), 92.

3. While many theologians have shared Aquinas's reasoning, others have taken diverging views. For example, the second-century theologian Irenaeus argued that Jesus ministered into his *forties*. See Alexander Robertson and James Donaldson, eds., *Irenaeus*, vol. 1, Ante-Nicene Library, book 2, chap. 22, verse 5 (Edinburgh: T & T Clark, 1884), 241.

4. Lewis R. Aiken, *Human Development in Adulthood* (New York: Plenum Press, 1998), 27.

5. W. Somerset Maugham, cited in James H. Schulz and Robert H. Binstock, *Aging Nation: The Economics and Politics of Growing Older in America* (Baltimore: Johns Hopkins University Press, 2006), 1.

6. Timothy Beatley, *Native to Nowhere: Sustaining Home and Community in a Global Age* (Washington, DC: Island Press, 2004), 272.

Question 7: Will We All Be Beautiful?

1. On this point I recommend Peter Kreeft's interesting chapter, "Is There Sex in Heaven?" *Everything You Wanted to Know about Heaven but Never Dreamed of Asking* (San Francisco: Ignatius, 1990), 117–32.

2. Naomi Wolf, *The Beauty Myth* (Toronto, Canada: Vintage, 1990), 12.

3. Jennifer O'Dea, "Preliminary Findings from the National Youth Cultures of Eating Study: Gender, Social Class and Ethnic Differences in Childhood Obesity," in Dorothy Bottrell and Gabrielle Meagher, eds., *Communities and Change: Selected Papers* (Sydney, Australia: Sydney University Press, 2008), 96.

4. Tertullian, "On the Flesh of Christ," in *The Writings of Tertullian II*, Ante-Nicene Christian Library, vol. 15, ed. Alexander Roberts and James Donaldson, trans. Peter Holmes (Edinburgh: T & T Clark, 1870), 186.

5. Incidentally, John's description of Jesus in Revelation 1:9–20 is too symbolic to glean anything about Jesus's postascension physical appearance beyond his undeniable glory. Nor does Stephen's vision in Acts 7:54–60 yield any useable information.

6. Cited in Joyce Tydesley, *Cleopatra: Last Queen of Egypt* (New York: Basic Books, 2008), 63.

7. Ibid.

8. On this point I think the lyrics of "I Don't Know How to Love Him," sung by Mary Magdalene in *Jesus Christ Superstar*, capture something of the unique and perplexing attraction of Jesus at a level far more profound than mere physical appeal.

Question 8: Will Anyone Be Deaf?

1. The promise of healing for the deaf is also mentioned in Old Testament passages like Isaiah 29:18, 42:18, and 43:8.

2. Carol Padden and Tom Humphries, *Deaf in America: Voices from a Culture* (Cambridge: Harvard University Press, 1988), 2.

3. Padden and Humphries observe that "in nearly every nation in the world there are several distinct groups of deaf people, their differences marked by political, historical, or geographical separation," Ibid., 3.

4. Padden and Humphries, *Deaf in America*, 8–9.

5. *Sound and Fury*, directed by Josh Aronson (New York: Aronson Film Associates, 2000).

6. Wayne Morris, *Theology without Words: Theology in the Deaf Society*, Explorations in Practical, Pastoral, and Empirical Theology Series (Aldershot, UK: Ashgate, 2008), 152.

7. Ibid., 151.

Question 9: Will We Still Get Thirsty, Hungry, and Sleepy?

1. Catherine A. Sanderson, *Social Psychology* (Hoboken, NJ: Wiley, 2010), 156.

2. Martin Luther, *Selected Works of Martin Luther*, vol. 1, trans. Henry Cole (London: Bensley, 1826), 290.

3. Ray Meddis, *The Sleep Instinct* (London: Routledge and Kegan Paul, 1977), 1.

Queston 10: Will There Be Sweet Melancholy?

1. Sally Brampton, *Shoot the Damn Dog: A Memoir of Depression* (New York: Norton, 2008), 18.

2. Mary Hays, *Memoirs of Emma Courtney*, ed. Marilyn L. Brooks (Peterborough, ON: Broadview Press, 2000), 317.

3. Emile M. Cioran, *On the Heights of Despair*, trans. Ilinca Zarifopol-Johnston (Chicago: University of Chicago Press, 1992), 32.

4. Ibid., 41.

5. Ibid.

6. Ibid., 31.

7. James W. Manns, *Aesthetics* (New York: Sharpe, 1998), 108.

Question 11: Will the *Titanic* Sail Again?

1. "Ships," in Geoffrey Bromiley, ed., *The International Standard Bible Encyclopedia*, vol. 4, Q–Z, rev. ed. (Grand Rapids: Eerdmans, 1988), 483.

2. Ibid.

Question 12: Will God Resurrect Entire Cultural Neighborhoods?

1. Jon Coe and Greg Dykstra, "New and Sustainable Directions in Zoo Design," in Devra G. Kleiman, Katerina V. Thompson, and Charlotte Kirk Baer, *Wild Animals in Captivity: Principles and Techniques for Zoo Management*, 2nd ed. (Chicago: University of Chicago Press, 2010), 214.

2. Nathan Rabin, *The Big Rewind: A Memoir Brought to You by Pop Culture* (New York: Simon and Schuster, 2009), 117–18.

3. Ibid., 122.

4. Cited in Joshua M. Greenberg, *From Betamax to Blockbuster: Video Stores and the Invention of Movies on Video* (Boston: MIT Press, 2008), 86.

5. Ibid., 88.

6. Rabin, *The Big Rewind*, 119.

Question 13: Will God Resurrect Insects?

1. James C. Dobson, *Stories of the Heart and Home* (Nashville: Word, 2000), 177.

2. Ibid.

3. *With Love, From Michigan: The Students of Highview Elementary School* (Lincoln, NE: School Success Press, 2002), 52.

4. George MacDonald, *Unspoken Sermons* (New York: Cosimo, 2007), 408.

5. See Philip J. King and Lawrence E. Stager, *Life in Biblical Israel* (Louisville: Westminster John Knox, 2001), 83, 118–19.

6. Timothy Duane Schowalter, *Insect Ecology: An Ecosystem Approach*, 2nd ed. (Burlington, MA: Academic Press, 2009), 234.

7. C. S. Lewis, *The Problem of Pain* (New York: HarperOne, 1996), 141.

8. Arthur V. Evans and Charles L. Bellamy, *An Inordinate Fondness for Beetles* (Berkeley: University of California Press, 2000), 9.

9. Ibid.

10. P. W. Price, et al., *Insect Ecology: Behavior, Populations and Communities* (Cambridge: Cambridge University Press, 2011), 8.

11. Ibid., 9.

12. See "Silence of the Bees: Impact of CCD on Agriculture," *Nature*, www.pbs.org/wnet/nature/episodes/silence-of-the-bees/impact-of-ccd-on-us-agriculture/37/.

13. Jonathan Edwards, "The Spider Letter," in John E. Smith, Harry S. Stout, and Kenneth P. Minkema, eds., *A Jonathan Edwards Reader* (New Haven: Yale Nota Bene, 2003), 1.

14. Ibid., 2.

15. Ibid., 5.

Question 14: Will Tigers Still Hunt Wild Boar?

1. Kate DiCamillo, *The Tiger Rising* (Cambridge, MA: Candlewick, 2001), 1–2.

2. Ibid., 99.

3. Ibid., 107–8.

4. Christopher Wright, *The God I Don't Understand* (Grand Rapids: Zondervan, 2008), 205.

5. George Adamson, quoted in Jeffrey Moussaieff Masson and Susan McCarthy, *When Elephants Weep: The Emotional Lives of Animals* (New York: Delta, 1995), xviii.

6. C. S. Lewis, *The Lion, the Witch and the Wardrobe* (New York: Scholastic, 1995), 80.

7. DiCamillo, *The Tiger Rising*. For further discussion, see Christopher Southgate, *The Groaning of Creation: God, Evolution, and the Problem of Evil* (Louisville: Westminster John Knox, 2008).

Question 15: Will We Walk with Jesus in the Garden?

1. Charles Austin Miles, "In the Garden," gospel song written in 1912, public domain.

2. Max Lucado, *Grace for the Moment*, vol. 1 (Nashville: J. Countryman, 2000), 348.

3. William Paul Young, *The Shack* (Newbury Park, CA: Windblown Media, 2007).

4. For further discussion of accommodation see question 1.

5. Philip Yancey, *The Jesus I Never Knew* (Grand Rapids: Zondervan, 1995), 39.

6. Young, *The Shack*, 110.

7. Ibid., 85, 219.

8. See my discussion in *Finding God in the Shack* (Colorado Springs: Biblica, 2009), 61–65.

Question 16: Will We Love Everyone the Same, or Will We Have Special Friends?

1. Joni Eareckson Tada, *Heaven: Your Real Home* (Grand Rapids: Zondervan, 1995), 49.

2. Bennett Helm, "Friendship," *Stanford Encyclopedia of Philosophy*, http://plato. stanford.edu/entries/friendship/.

3. Ibid.

Question 17: Will We Find Intelligent Aliens There?

1. Roger Ebert, review of *Contact* in *Chicago Sun-Times*, http://rogerebert.sun times.com/apps/pbcs.dll/article?AID=/19970711/REVIEWS/707110301/1023.

2. Paul Davies, *God and the New Physics* (New York: Simon and Shuster, 1983), 71.

3. See Mark Clark, Hugh Ross, and Kenneth Samples, *Lights in the Sky and Little Green Men* (Colorado Springs: NavPress, 2002), chap. 4.

4. In his science fiction novel *Perelandra*, C. S. Lewis describes a planet of unfallen, humanlike creatures.

5. Larry Norman, "UFO," *In Another Land*, Solid Rock Records, 1976.

6. See the discussion in Thomas F. O'Meara, O. P., "Christian Theology and Extraterrestrial Intelligent Life," *Theological Studies*, vol. 60 (1999): 3–30.

7. For a good introduction to the debate, see Dennis L. Okholm and Timothy R. Phillips, eds., *Four Views on Salvation in a Pluralistic World* (Grand Rapids: Zondervan, 1996).

8. See George A. Lindbeck, *The Nature of Doctrine: Religion and Theology in a Postliberal Age* (Louisville: Westminster John Knox, 1984), 59.

9. Perhaps only those aliens who will freely receive the gospel once it is proclaimed to them will be offered a second chance to hear it in a glorified creation.

Question 18: Will We Still Have Free Will?

1. Clark H. Pinnock, *Most Moved Mover: A Theology of God's Openness* (Carlisle, UK: Paternoster; Grand Rapids: Baker Academic, 2001), 7, emphasis added.

2. See Simon Francis Gaine, *Will There Be Free Will in Heaven? Freedom, Impeccability, and Beatitude* (London: T & T Clark, 2003), 1.

3. See Stephen Sakur, "Eating Christmas Trees at 'the World's Best Restaurant,'" *BBC News Magazine*, www.bbc.co.uk/news/magazine-16440034.

4. "Two Buck Chuck" is the slang term for Charles Shaw Winery's (until recently) two-dollar bottle of wine.

Question 19: If My Child Goes to Hell, Will I Know and Will I Care?

1. Tertullian, cited in William Barclay, *The Revelation of John*, vol. 2, rev. ed., The Daily Study Bible (Burlington, Ontario, Canada: Welch, 1976), 12.

2. Aquinas is assuming the contrast effect that I discussed in Question 9.

3. See Thomas Aquinas, *Summa Theologiae*, supplement to III, Q. 94, Art. 1–3.

4. Lars Svendsen, *A Philosophy of Evil*, trans. Kerry A. Pierce (Champaign, IL: Dalkey Archive Press, 2010), 103.

5. David L. Edwards and John Stott, *Evangelical Essentials: A Liberal-Evangelical Dialogue* (Downers Grove, IL: InterVarsity Press, 1988), 312.

6. Svendsen, *A Philosophy of Evil*, 104, emphasis added.

7. John Portman, *When Bad Things Happen to Other People* (New York: Routledge, 2000), 197.

8. Some Christians object that invoking thick descriptions in this kind of discussion is emotionally manipulative. On the contrary, I believe that appealing to emotionally compelling narratives can often help us clarify moral issues. See my blog post, "Free Will, Hell, and Reasonable Appeals to Emotion," June 6, 2011, http://randalrauser.com/2011/06/free-will-hell-and-reasonable-appeals-to-emotion/.

Question 20: Should We Hope That Everyone Will Be Saved?

1. For a defense of universalism, see Gregory MacDonald, *The Evangelical Universalist* (Eugene, OR: Cascade, 2006). For a helpful primer to the debate, see Robin A. Parry and Christopher H. Partridge, eds., *Universal Salvation? The Current Debate* (Grand Rapids, and Cambridge, UK: Eerdmans, 2003).

2. Roger Ebert, review of *The Woodsman*, http://rogerebert.suntimes.com/apps/pbcs.dll/article?AID=/20050106/REVIEWS/50103001/1023.

3. Edwards and Stott, *Evangelical Essentials*, 314.

Randal Rauser (PhD, King's College London) is associate professor of historical theology at Taylor Seminary, Edmonton, Canada. He is the author or coauthor of several books, including *God or Godless?*, *Finding God in the Shack*, and *The Swedish Atheist, the Scuba Diver, and Other Apologetic Rabbit Trails*. He is a popular speaker who seeks to bring the truth of Scripture to bear on today's real-life issues. He lives in Alberta and blogs at www.randalrauser.com.

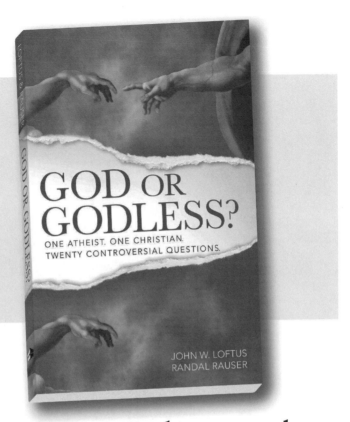